THE SOUTHERN POETRY ANTHOLOGY

VOLUME V

GEORGIA

FIRST EDITION, 2012

Requests for permission to reproduce material from this work should be sent to:

Permissions
Texas Review Press
English Department
Sam Houston State University
Huntsville, TX 77341-2146

Cover design and photo by Chad M. Pelton

Erratum:

Angelle Scott's poem, "The Men Who Sit Under the Trees" was supposed to appear in Volume IV, Louisiana. My apologies to the poet and to readers of the series.

A brief word about the below information: The Library of Congress directed us to use the CIP data from the first volume of the anthology, even though we have distinct data for volumes two and three. The correct publication information is listed below, before this data:

Title: The Southern Poetry Anthology, V: Georgia
Editors: William Wright and Paul Ruffin
ISBN-13: 978-1-933896-93-9
ISBN-10: 1-933896-93-9

Library of Congress Cataloging-in-Publication Data

The Southern poetry anthology : South Carolina / [compiled] by Stephen Gardner and
William Wright ~ 1st ed.
      p. cm.
   ISBN-13: 978-1-933896-06-9 (pbk. : alk. paper)
   ISBN-10: 1-933896-06-X (pbk : alk. paper)
   1. American poetry~South Carolina. I. Gardner, Stephen. II. Wright, William, 1979-
   PS558.S6S68 2007
   811.008'09757~dc22
                     2007023711

THE SOUTHERN POETRY ANTHOLOGY

VOLUME V

GEORGIA

William Wright, *Series Editor*

Paul Ruffin & William Wright, *Volume Editors*

PREVIOUS VOLUMES

William Wright, Series Editor

Volume I: South Carolina
Edited by Stephen Gardner and William Wright

ISBN-10: 193389606X
ISBN-13: 978-1933896069

Volume II: Mississippi
Edited by Stephen Gardner and William Wright

ISBN-10: 1933896248
ISBN-13: 978-1933896243

Volume III: Contemporary Appalachia
Edited by Jesse Graves, Paul Ruffin, and William Wright

ISBN-10: 1933896647
ISBN-13: 978-1933896649

Volume IV: Louisiana
Edited by Paul Ruffin and William Wright

ISBN-10: 1933896779
ISBN-13: 9781933896779

FORTHCOMING

Volume VI: Tennessee (2013)
Edited by Jesse Graves, Paul Ruffin, and William Wright

The editors dedicate this volume
to Georgia poets,
past, present, and future

Foreword

As of its fall 2012 printing, this is the single largest volume of *The Southern Poetry Anthology* to date—not in terms of page count—but, more significantly, in terms of the number of poets included. For a matter of comparison: The third volume, celebrating poets of contemporary Appalachia, an entire *sub-region*, is a smaller book. This abundance reveals the numerous literary groups and close-knit communities all over Georgia—Augusta, Macon, Valdosta, Atlanta, Douglasville, Carrollton, the north Georgia mountains, the myriad small towns, the coast, and elsewhere. Too, my wife and I live in Marietta, now, and thus have had the privilege to work with many writers in Atlanta and surrounding areas, and the variegation of styles and textures, as well as the number of truly dedicated and gifted poets, is almost dizzying. In my private workshops, I am consistently astounded by my participants' dedication, seriousness, and kindness. And I am heartened to know that many similar workshops and community celebrations of poetry persist, indeed thrive, throughout the state.

I am proud of this edition, proud that it includes such established authors as Natasha Trethewey, David Bottoms, Kevin Young, Thomas Lux, Alice Friman, Stephen Corey, Memye Curtis Tucker, Judson Mitchum, Gregory Fraser, Chad Davidson, Kathryn Stripling Byer, T.R. Hummer, and many others. I am proud, too, that many of these poets are editors themselves—Roberta George, Kevin Cantwell, Dan Veach, and James Malone Smith, just to name a few—who understand the difficult but rewarding work involved in ushering a work such as this into print. Perhaps most of all, I love sharing new, genuinely gifted poets such as Christopher Martin, Erin Ganaway, and Jo Brachman with a potentially wide readership. Of course I value the myriad other wonderful poets in this anthology, whose work creates, individually and taken together, a beautiful music. I appreciate that I have been given the opportunity to meet and interact with a great many of these contributors, to become part of the community this anthology celebrates.

I would like to thank Pat Landreth Keller and Starkey Flythe,who helped locate wonderful poets throughout the state for Paul Ruffin and me. Thanks to Leon Stokesbury for his introduction, and, by extension, his own anthology of southern poetry, *The Made Thing: An Anthology of Contemporary Southern Poetry*, one of the first inspirations for this entire series. I would like to thank David Bottoms, Robert Morgan, James Seay, Betty Adcock, Charles Wright, and Jack Butler for igniting in me the desire to become a writer. The *Southern Poetry Anthology* would not exist without them. Robert Penn Warren, Vassar Miller, and James Dickey were also part of this formative catalyst.

Most of all, I would like to thank the contributors, who made this edition a truly special one, a milestone for the series. I hope you enjoy getting to know your Georgia neighbors as much as I have.

William Wright
Marietta, Georgia

Introduction

Surely, this is God's plenty. And so I feel I need to begin with a few facts of my own. I have lived in the American South always, and in Georgia for the past twenty-five years. My principal interest all my adult life has been the writing, teaching, and study of contemporary poetry. Thus, I have come to consider myself as a sort of "expert" in the field of contemporary Southern Poetry. I even published a couple of anthologies on the subject. So, it was with some surprise that I read this manuscript and realized that I was unfamiliar with the work of most of the poets included herein. It was a new and wonderful experience to come across so much new material of such a high quality by so many new voices. What better evidence that the poetry of Georgia is healthy and growing stronger?

In truth, the history of Georgia poetry before the last forty or fifty years is not particularly distinguished. Robert Penn Warren lived elsewhere, as did John Crowe Ransom and the other Agrarians. The deciding figures in Southern literature were fiction writers, at least for the first two-thirds of the twentieth century. And it was William Faulkner above everyone else, a bit perhaps like Zeus, who defined and dominated Southern literature. His influence is almost impossible to overemphasize. No one else has excelled to such a degree in each of what have come to be considered the two or three principal attributes in the field. He placed his stories in the rural center of Nature, creating the conflicts that man's emersion in such an environment would be sure to generate. He added the sense of defeat and loss, originally stemming from the losses of the Civil War, but growing into a statement about the innate nature of the human condition. And it was Faulkner who shaded this into the various aspects of Southern Gothic and decadence that permeates so much of Southern fiction and poetry, even today. None of this is unique to the South. It is all a matter of emphasis and flavor. And in this regard, Georgia does have major figures that have had considerable influence on fiction and poetry.

It was not until the emergence of James Dickey in the sixties that the state had a poet of such significance that his influence was, and is, still discernible. Influenced by the great nature poets, Wordsworth, Emerson, and Roethke, Dickey added his Southern twist of darkness, an attempt to achieve some true union with the world outside one's self. Combined with place and voice, the disturbing nature behind such gothic union in poems like "The Sheep Child," "The Shark's Parlor," "Falling," and many others, gave an entirely new and simultaneously decadent turn to Georgia and Southern poetry.

Perhaps Southern and Georgia poetry's most apparent attribute has been its being centered in the pastoral and rural nature of our region. This is still the case but, as the reader turns these pages, this is not so as much as it once was. This should not surprise. The last twenty years, the period with which many of these poems are concerned, as well as when most of them were written, has seen an encroachment of technology move into people's lives unlike anything in history. Any regional art is dependent, at least to some degree, on the insular quality of the region. New technology continues to create such a fury and froth of connections that it would be naïve to suppose that it is not having some homogenizing effect on every aspect of modern life, including regional literature. I am not sure if this is a good thing or a bad thing, but it is happening, and the future is not what it used to be. But given the quality of the poetry that comes out of this flux, evident in this anthology, it seems fine to me. And even so, it's easy to find many of these poems still tied to the land—Athens, Cherokee County, Okefenokee, Woodruff Park, and Macon, too: specificity of place, and the subjects found there.

Whether Sutpens, or Compsons, or Snopes, Faulkner's fiction is filled with the personal histories of families going back into the mid-nineteenth century and the huge defeat always lurking there. And his characters in the more-or-less present are constantly being drawn back into their own family's past and caught there forever. Paradoxically, the past does not exist; it cannot be regained; and yet all of us are bound to travel the same roads trying to regain what we cannot. Literary characters are placed in profoundly dramatic plots that accentuate the hopelessness of our place in time, and novelists are free to manipulate them as they wish.

But the genre of poetry provides a different means of approaching this subject. The main character of most poetry is the poet writing the poem. So the personal history, the place in Time, and usually the characters involved, are meant to be perceived as real. The poet is often the subject matter, and the poem is often written in the first person. And if it is written in the third person, then it concerns some real relative, a grandfather, or grandmother, or sister, or mother, or, as is often the case, a father. The poet is a person trying to understand the self through personal history. This endeavor fails, but it seems to be all the poet has. There are many examples of such poems in Southern literature. Warren and Ransom certainly possess some of the most wonderful creations in this regard. Allen Tate's "The Swimmers" is likewise as much as one could wish for such a poem. More recently, Dickey's "The Hospital Window," among others, carries the tradition forward. And in what we might call contemporary Southern poetry, there are others, such as the work Miller Williams and Frank Stanford from Arkansas. I know of no better example of the Georgia poetry of personal history than David Bottoms' poems in this book about his coming to grips with his relationship with his father. So this is an attribute of Southern poetry still active, even flourishing.

Finally, there is a perhaps new poetic theme or tone that should be mentioned here. I find it curling round a number of poems in this anthology. It is new to Southern poetry, and not really part of the tradition, but it does seem to have made its noticeable appearance over the last twenty years or so, not just in the South but all over the country. There is a species of wit that has come into its own as a means of dealing with or understanding this too-fast world. I sometimes think it comes from the point of view of someone thinking, "You better laugh, because the alternative is much less palpable." In America, certain poets of the sixties began to perceive the world this way, absurdist visions that suggest anything is possible (as there is no proof of meaning anywhere). James Tate and Russell Edson were some of the first exponents of this, influenced by earlier European and South American voices. But contemporary southern poetry has its own practitioners: Tony Hoagland and R.S. Gwynn in Texas, and Everette Maddox in Louisiana, are some of the most successful.

Georgia too is feeling the influence of this "unsouthern" theme. For example, Mac Gay's lament for Pluto's recent demotion, "Pluto's Despair," found within this anthology, is a poem that no one else would have written by someone few have heard of. It is a unique expression of a unique mind caught in a unique moment:

> Heck, here you've been
> a-list for years, part and
> parcel of the pantheon,
> "one of the nine best ever,"
> According to the old Almanac
> of Science, and though
> nowhere near the largest,
> certainly the most distant,
> the most cryptic and aloof,
> secluded in the hinterlands,
> enigmatic as Salinger.

And such moments take many forms. Chelsea Rathburn, a quite different poet in a number of ways, can take her own memories and apply a similar technique to wring this uniqueness out of them, in a poem like "Fire Ants:"

> What happened next? What curses did I utter?
> And how did I ever get back over the fence?
> I remember having a kind of reverence
> for the whole affair: the pity I got, each bite
> growing large and lustrous as a pearl, my tight
> and swollen toes. I must have liked the pain.
> What else would make me prod again, again?

In seemingly effortless loose heroic couplets, Rathburn applies not only wit, but one of the oldest of traditional forms to her capturing, in the present, this moment from her past.

In my end as in my beginning, the bottom line is still the fact that a multitude of new voices is creating a multitude of very fine poems in Georgia. Are they in the same tradition and styles as the Southern poetry of the past? Sometimes. But so many new forces are washing into our poetry now that it seems that the best approach to such flux is to be glad and to embrace those forces, to contain multitudes. So many other things are happening, and being written, that a new village of poets thrives throughout Georgia. And the editors of this anthology have indeed performed their duty well, for it is a garland of flowers, beautiful and more multicolored than anyone might have imagined, and a most wonderful way to spend some afternoons and feel the earth made new again.

Leon Stokesbury
Tucker, Georgia

Contents

Holly J. Alderman
18   *Rabbit Tree*

Diane Anhalt
19   *Street Scene with Poet*

Rebecca Baggett
20   *Chestnut*
21   *Heaven*

Fred Bassett
23   *Accidents*
24   *Vultures*

Kimberly Becker
25   *Dahlonega*

Marjorie Becker
26   *Sea-green Ease*
26   *Capturing Sighs and Gemstones in Bundles, in Baskets*

Hannah Bessinger
28   *Sunflower*

Jenn Blair
29   *Collect*
29   *Red Clay Christ*

Maggie Blake
30   *I Tried*

Julie E. Bloemeke
31   *Clock Work*

Stephen Bluestone
32   *Wheels*
34   *The Flagrant Dead*
36   *The Unveiling*

David Bottoms
37   *Under the Vulture-Tree*
38   *The Desk*
40   *A Chat With My Father*

J.O. Brachman
41   *Lightning Bug Phenomenon*

Jesse Breite
42   *Highway 40*

Molly Brodak
43   *Drawings of Ships*
44   *Landscapes*

Jody Brooks
45   *Stealing Strawberries*

Brian Brown
46   A Brief History of the Wiregrass

Stacey Lynn Brown
47   Excerpts from Cradle Song: Sections I, II, and XXVII

Kathryn Stripling Byer
50   Coastal Plains
51   Scuppernongs
52   Gone Again

Melisa Cahnmann-Taylor
53   Goldkist Poultry, Athens, Georgia
54   In the Name of God

Brent Calderwood
55   Nocturne
56   Rain

Kevin Cantwell
57   The Next Abstinence
58   Night Game Vexed by a Line from Melville
59   One of Those Russian Novels

Michelle Castleberry
60   A Man's World, 1966
61   Bounty

Katie Chaple
62   Pretty Little Rooms
63   Gross Anatomy

Elizabeth J. Colen
64   Little Bird

Stephen Corey
65   Abjuring Political Poetry
66   Emily Dickinson Considers Basketball
67   Universe

Daniel Corrie
68   World's Time
69   The Years
70   Money

Chad Davidson
72   Target
73   Cleopatra's Bra
75   Ginkgo

Travis Denton
77   Burden of Speech
78   Local Men

Michael Diebert
79   Dream Songs: Summer, Atlanta

Maudelle Driskell
82   The Propaganda of Memory
82   The Heart's Archaeology

Blanche Farley
83   *Alder Moon*
84   *Good Friday in Jasper*
85   *Laughter*

Malaika Favorite
86   *The End*

Rupert Fike
87   *First Memory, Grandfather's Cabin*
88   *Commune Winter*
89   *Radical Rhetoric, 1968*

Starkey Flythe, Jr.
90   *Greeks*
91   *Among the Things We Had*
92   *We're Taking the Real Estate Exam*

Ethan Fogus
93   *Shadow*

Gregory Fraser
94   *End of Days*
96   *The Stuff*
97   *Poetry Is Stupid*

Kerri French
99   *Dear Hands*
100   *Tobacco*

Alice Friman
101   *Troubled Interiors*
102   *Visiting Flannery*
103   *The Night I Saw Saturn*

Erin Ganaway
104   *Passing*
105   *Sea Cleft*
106   *Crustose*

Mac Gay
107   *Pluto's Despair*

Roberta George
108   *Three o*

Sarah Gordon
110   *Narrative*
111   *Acts of Love*
112   *A Call to Prophecy*

G.R. Greenbaum
114   *At the Gates of Dachau*

Sîan Griffiths
115   *Fistful*
116   *Proud Flesh*
117   *Persistence of Geese*

Anthony Grooms
118   *In Rousseau's Garden*
119   *The Slave Houses at Green Springs, Virginia*

Linda Lee Harper
120   *Final Cut*

Karen Head
121   *Part of the Bargain*

M. Ayodele Heath
122   *On Closing Woodruff Park, Atlanta*
124   *Eye of the Beholder*

Sara Henning
125   *Eros*

Lisa Hodgens
126   *When You Come*
127   *Uweyv Nyva*

Karen Paul Holmes
128   *Singing with Beethoven*

Randall Horton
129   *Wail the Sinner*

James Hudson
130   *The Feel of Fall*

T.R. Hummer
131   *Slow Train Through Georgia*
132   *Friendly Fire*
133   *Apocatastasis Foretold in the Shape of a Canvas of Smoke*

Mike James
135   *I Used to Dream of Becoming the Village Idiot*

Christopher Jelley
136   *Barrier Island*

Gordon Johnston
137   *Bear*
138   *Crutches*
139   *Hooters Girls*

Seaborn Jones
140   *Semper Fi*
141   *Telephoning Ginsberg*
143   *Lost Keys, Coffee and Guns*

Melanie Jordan
145   *Ghost Season*
146   *A Mural in the Abandoned Cane Hill Asylum*

Pat Landreth Keller
148   *Draglines*
150   *The Woman at the Window*
151   *Not for Publication*

Collin Kelley
153   The Virgin Mary Appears in a Highway Underpass
154   Three Mile Island

Anthony Kellman
155   Early Birds
156   Epiphany through a Small Town

Bill King
157   Crow Addresses the Mythmakers
158   The Pond

David King
159   Dusk at the Starlight Drive-In
160   Night Trains

Hilary King
161   I Do Not Have Mary Oliver's Apple Tree

Alyse Knorr
162   Alice Recalls Georgia to Jenny

Robert Krut
163   Walking Toward the Blue Song
164   Being Somewhere I Shouldn't

Joshua Lavender
165   The Death of Auntie Bellum's Attic

Kathleen Brewin Lewis
167   Whereupon the Writer Thinks She Is the Center of the Universe

Cody Lumpkin
168   Cooking Spam Outdoors
169   Squirrel Metaphysics

Thomas Lux
170   Refrigerator, 1957
171   Beneath the Apple Branches Bent Dumbly
172   There Were Some Summers

Dan Marshall
173   Koan

Christopher Martin
174   Antidote to Narcissus
174   Revelation on the Cherokee County Line

James May
175   Natural Grief
176   The Reddened Flower, the Erotic Bird
177   Fringe Tree

mariana mcdonald
178   Father's Day, Lake Pontchartrain

Sandra Meek
179   Acacia karroo Hayne (White Thorn)
180   Coma
182   Tillandsia Usneoides

Judson Mitcham
184   Night
185   Praise
186   Tennessee

Maren O. Mitchell
187   The Sensual Art of Tomato Slicing

Janice Townley Moore
188   Evening Out
189   Teaching the Robins
190   Note to the King of Green Lawn Service

Tony Morris
191   Blue Iris
193   Reflectors
194   Something about Chickens

Ginger Murchison
195   Songwriter
196   The Orchid
197   Guilt

Alicia Rebecca Myers
198   Insomnia

Eric Nelson
199   Fair Road
200   The Lowcountry
201   In Another Year

Robert Parham
202   The Concept of Why
204   The Dark Car Enters
205   The First Scaffold

Amy Pence
206   8th Grade Locker Combination

Patricia Percival
207   Beam

Patrick Phillips
208   Nathaniel
210   My Lovely Assistant
211   Blueridge Bestiary

David Scott Pointer
213   Film Time Flash to the Future

Stephen Roger Powers
214   The Great Chicago Earthquake of 2002

Wyatt Prunty
215   Fields
216   The Combine
217   Late Walks

Chelsea Rathburn
218   Raft of Grief
219   The Talker
219   Fire Ants

Janisse Ray
220   Secret
221   Okefenokee Swamp
222   Land of Milk and Honey

Billy Reynolds
224   The Unfledged Ducks in the Abandoned Clarifier
226   Easter Garden

Jonathan Rice
227   Passover
230   Folie a Deux
232   The Least of Us

Ann Ritter
234   Toward Solstice
235   Etude
236   Mulberry, Burnt Orange, Pistachio

Liz Robbins
237   Studio

Dan Rosenberg
238   New Idioms
239   Heaven

Rosemary Rhodes Royston
240   On the Discovery of Aspirin

Jenny Sadre-Orafai
241   Foiled Season

Angelle Scott
242   The Men Who Sit Under the Trees

M.E. Silverman
243   The Mud Angel of Macon
244   Separation Grows
245   Why There Is No Fifth Season

James Malone Smith
247   Frequencies
248   The Boathouse
249   The Captive

Leon Stokesbury
250   The Day Kennedy Died
252   Nemerov's "A Primer of the Daily Round" Held as a Mirror Up to Nature
254   Watching My Mother Take Her Last Breath

Alice Teeter
255   Stones

Kathleen Thompson
256   Lament

Natasha Trethewey
257   Elegy
259   Knowledge
260   On Captivity

Rachel Trousdale
262   Lost in the Woods

Memye Curtis Tucker
263   Ghosts
264   Radishes
265   Dusk in College Park

Mimi Vaquer
266   Ode to a Fence

Kevin Vaughn
267   Home Opener
268   New Way Cleaners
269   Metamorphosis

Dan Veach
272   Ancient of Nights

William Walsh
274   My Grandfather's Christmas Tree

Betsy Weir
275   For a Child Leaving Home

Kelly Whiddon
276   Thumbing for a Hitch
277   Dirty Glass

Austin Wilson
278   Snake Season

Edward Wilson
279   Boy
279   Smoke knows

Ralph Tejeda Wilson
280   The Little Deaths

William Wright
281   Blonde Mare, Iredell Co., N.C., 1870-1896

Caroline Young
282   Forty

Kevin Young
284   James Brown at B.B. King's on New Year's Eve
285   Ode to Ol Dirty Bastard
287   Relics

288   The Poets

Holly J. Alderman

Rabbit Tree

Its
low
boughs
are
gang planks
over
a rolling sea
of clover,
where
nectar-drunk bees
stumble
amid white flowers.
A child
can part its limbs,
wedge herself into the shade
and pretend
she's a rabbit
escaping heat in the voiceless verdure.
With ears so sensitive
she counts breaking vows. . . deserting footsteps. . .
that even the bees' carousing or a dragonfly's hum
can't drown.

Diana Anhalt

Street Scene with Poet

Here, at the corner of *'Revolución'* and Altavista,
the longest stoplight in Mexico City, the lottery
vendor stations himself in front of my car: *'Siete,
siete, número de suerte'*–Seven, seven, lucky seven.
I watch a child, two balloons stuffed into the seat
of her tights, clamber up her father's back, perch
on his shoulders, waggle her hips, stand on one leg–
and catch my breath. The woman who sells cigarettes,
two or three at a time, knocks on my window. Today,
the one-armed trumpet player and his wife have not
arrived. The *'tragafuegos'* has. He lights his torch,
pours gasoline into his mouth, spits toward his flame.

That's when the old man, hunkered in his wheelchair,
spots me, doffs his sombrero and labors through traffic.
From here, the smog-fuzzed trees appear to float, pencil
scrawls hastily erased. I switch off the radio–Bach's
Brandenburg Concerto. I roll down my window–breathe
in the smell of backed-up drainage, burnt rubber. *'Hola
niña bonita.'* He pulls out a notebook. *Today I wrote
some poetry just for you. I call it 'Mi Cantar,' My Song.*
Two kids in low-slung jeans haunt my car–I place
my bag beneath my seat. *'Ayer escribí de angelitos.
Hoy escribo del amor.'* Yesterday I wrote of angels.

Today I write of love. He squints down at his notes.
En el silencio del amanecer recuerdo a mi querida.
In the silence of dawn I remember my belovéd. Church
bells clamor, horns pummel the air. *Be my moon,
be my sun.* A stray mutt shuffles past, nuzzles his crotch.
He starts again: *'Ayer escribí de angelitos. Hoy escribo
del amor. . . .* The driver behind me steps on his throttle,
honks his horn, hurls an insult out his window: *¡Muevete
vieja pendeja!* Traffic wheezes to a start. *Adios, gracias.*
I thrust a ten peso coin in the old man's direction. *'Ven mañana,
señorita.'* Come tomorrow, tomorrow I'll have something new.

Rebecca Baggett

Chestnut

I touched a chestnut sapling
in the Georgia mountains.

My friend writes of the great trees
and their vanishing,

but I have seen a young chestnut,
tender and green, rising from its ashes.

I, too, write of loss and grief,
the hollow they carve

in the chest,
but that hollow may shelter

some new thing,
a life I could not

have imagined or wished,
a life I would never

have chosen. I have seen
the chestnut rising,

luminous,
from its own bones,

from the ash of its first life.

Heaven

for Pam and Debbie

I never could hope for heaven
though I knew I was expected

to desire it, not even when we heard
the Bible verses guaranteeing

many mansions, one for each of us
if we believed. I believed

and dreaded it: lone inhabitant
of white marble halls, immaculate,

echoing, austere, my sole escape
the streets of pearl and alabaster

where ranks of small angels fidgeted
with golden harps and droned Sunday school hymns

for all eternity. Perhaps I could appeal,
I thought, when my time came,

petition to stay here,
on my beloved dirty planet,

its dusty gray roads lined with forbidden ditches,
squelching and cool beneath bare feet,

home of red-capped mosses, ants' trails,
butterflies' quivering mosaic wings,

sand packed at the waves' margin,
shell-scattered, tunneled by fiddler crabs,

its sweet lazy summers tasting of sap
from sticky pink azalea blossoms,

tang of sour grass and clover
sucked while contemplating cloud-herds,

roadside berries weighting shirt hems,
sun-hot, summer-heavy, bittersweet,

and its crisp autumns, marked by bouquets
of goldenrod and roadside asters

and bonfires, blazing with this year's garden stalks,
whose bright embers we watched pop and rise

until they melted among the stars,
sure that Jesus and all the angels leaned down

to look on and envy us.

Fred Bassett

Accidents

Grace is the way out, you want to say
but don't, knowing how it sounds
when you're not the one who backed
the car over your two-year-old,
or killed your best friend on a hunting trip.
But I'm always empathic
and thankful too for the soft patch
of luck beneath my trembling feet.

Things were very good for a neighbor.
A second place in the country
with pastures for horses,
forests for beauty and firewood.
The chainsaw revved its sharp teeth
until the oak began to fall.
Timber, the father cried. The oak,
with a mind of its own, twisted
and lodged against a smaller hickory,
bending it like a giant bow
drawn to its limits. One whack
from his ax, and the hickory snaps
with a sharp backward thrust—
a missile locked on the daughter's head.
The living could not believe their eyes.

Only a lumberjack could have known.
That, I assured him often,
having once been a logger.
But would facts ease the sorrow?
Or even the drag of years?
Then the answer came with one loud report.

Vultures

The connotations are all negative,
but I've learned to admire the feathered ones.
Repulsed as a boy, I call them all buzzards
and kept my distance, until I disrupted
a good dozen, aground in the forest,
feasting on a bloated cow—
one backing out of a ragged hole
in the belly dragging the liver.

Now I think of vultures as the Jains
of the bird kingdom—never striking
a blow at a living thing. At first sight,
I pause to catch a defining feature
and breathe, turkey or black,
as the case may be. It's just my nod
to Nature's design that we alone,
of all species, deny with our entombments.

Kimberly Becker

Dahlonega

*Discovery of gold in 1828 led to the Georgia
gold rush that hastened the Trail of Tears*

When I say I'm going to Dahlonega,
and ask directions from the fellow
at the gas station, he says I say it wrong.
I say it the Cherokee way for yellow:

dalonige

The town's museum:
testament to greed,
land lotteried
Even the bricks wink and glitter in collusion

dalonige

An Indian friend says gold
is "the yellow rock that makes whites crazy"
We laugh although we hold
pain below our words

dalonige

You saw in me something of worth,
inherent wealth from birth
Go slow go slow my love
delve deep to treasures that I keep

dalonige

Dahlonega's gold was pure
before the California rush
There is no cure for desire,
pan filled with silt, with fool's

dalonige

When you say you want me,
my body already yields, vein on vein,
your mine, your land, your claim
Crazy for your touch, I become

dalonige

Marjorie Becker

Sea-green Ease

She wandered, this was Zamable,
the Mexican village named for her orchestra,
for her hidden and dense charities,
middle name, petticoats of the silken ago;
and she here, she taught indigenous women
and they her, how to hold a pencil, a *pluma*,
a knife, how to allow sea-green ease,
its inner color, light, to summon or release,
how to find in fact any color, lingering embrace
they sought, what imagination, after all,
might yield.

Capturing Sighs and Gemstones in Bundles, in Baskets

They lived in a small brick house,
a massive oak seizing the light,
no wisteria pods, shock of gardenia.
She spent her days dark-haired, pudgy,
the heat implacable, nobody aware,
she wandered out back, she wandered alone,
composing.

There would be babies aplenty,
She had no knowledge, just a sense from songs,
(her made-up songs, she never told) and
suddenly
walking past the swing set, whirligig, slide,
walking past a bricked-up oven, unused, unkempt,
she crouched down.
Anemones.
Four: purple, lilac, lavender, gold.
She'd never seen them; she was in love.
She wanted, always wanted that moment,

the sense that there is something,
the longing, still a longing,
she knew no one saw
nor the hours skating, dreaming of a little boy skating too,
capturing in bundles, in baskets,
the sudden emeralds, sapphires as they skated,
the years waiting, never saying,
the recognitions, there were anemones,
a day she went so black-haired, Jewish,
the day the other girls all shriven, she supposed,
or possibly late-comers, a Bible School Baptismal dunk,
there were anemones.

She waited, always waited
for a later-on love,
a person who would enter and quietly,
quietly trace the paths she'd made,
wander to their hilt, their height,
their instinct when unseen to flee,
the ways she leapt,
and the day she waited for, waits for still,
a homecoming,
anemones everywhere, harvested,
an inner path, the crystal markings,
songs leaping, tumbling from her throat,
colors filling a stoop and suddenly
lavender, lilac, purple, gold.

Hannah Bessinger

Sunflower

The full-blooded dusk sings spells
around this heavy lidded god eye;
guarding the garden gate
as a self-appointed watchman
who, while others sleep
witnesses the breaking free
of shoots from soil
moon from sky-glass
and one stray soul
from its body.

Jenn Blair

Collect

Dried dung from last summer's sold animals
at the auction yard. Houses hid in the trees,
red childless tricycle rusting. You wondering
who last sat in that faded couch left out now
for the crows, coils exposed, wire tresses
splayed, holy diadem of mouse nest. We were
passing through and so were thoughtful.
They were not our barns, not our falling apart
tool sheds. They were not our fields, half cut,
as the sun went down. The water in
the well—someone else's inheritance.
Our fathers tied bean vines far from
here; our mothers never found this soil
under their cracked nails. And that is how.
We were tricked into fondness at last.
We will die for it, but cannot help it.
The way we always love what is not ours
with such a fierce and particular pang.

Red Clay Christ

Christ—at one decibel: loud.
Christ large lettered, radiant
and reaching, His arms—clouds—covering
hills. Christ unabashed, and washed
in His own blood, and rising. Christ
shining-browed, barefooted and bringing
morning. Christ carrying the sword
that cuts all asunder, splitting cell from cell
even as He cleaves stranger to stranger,
startles green leaves into flaming tongues
clucking on the black walnut tree.

Maggie Blake

I Tried

The pull back waste of low tide.
Bait fish racing or
left behind, flipping, silver to sand
silver to sand, gasping with colder mouths.

Seaweed clinging to the shore,
only gaining ground
in a storm, hurled a little closer to home.

Doorframe, a lawn mower,
hurricane heaved, thrown
onto the path, taken
by a sea of eel grass.

Even eel grass bent in the wind
with its back turned white,
like bone, white like the crane

at the edge of the tide pool
facing just another crane.

Both, when in flight, resembling arrows.

Julie E. Bloemeke

Clock Work

Because it enters the body in sleep,
this thought of hands, of face,
this idea we must make round,
this ticking cycle of wait.

Because with only the cells
and organs awake, it buys
a new house, enters in.

Because the words begin
as anxious thought:
When?

Because the heart can't
help but anticipate, the
lonely mind can't help
but be young, yearning
for embrace, too shy to ask.

Because the soul needs
it, or this is what the
thought says. When really
it is all poetry, the want,
the wait, the acceptance
of hands.

.

Stephen Bluestone

Wheels

Before the Silver Ghost, the Maserati, Lamborghini,
the Marmon, Daimler, Napier, Pope-Hartford,
the stylish Panhard et Levassor, the boat-tail Packard,
the Wills Sainte Claire, the glittering Delahaye,
the pressed steel chassis, sleeve valves, chain drives,
the overhead cam, disc brakes, the fettled aluminum block
under the shining Bugatti bonnet, the plated levers,
the felt-lined mahogany floorboards with hold-down screws
in bronze bushings, the chrome-plated buttons,
the friction shocks, the flat-out speed, the noise
at all hours of the day and night, at all times of the year,
there had been, of course, the normal going back and forth
from Paris to Joinville, Cheltenham to Gloucester,
and Glasgow to Paisley. As always, the muddy roads,
the wagon ruts, the fordings, the crumbling stone bridges,
the collapsing masonry beneath the ancient crossings,
the overgrowth of trees, the herds in pasturage,
the flocks of sheep, defined the passage. When Napoleon
sent armies into Italy, he conquered mountains;
with certain passes paved, he changed a continent.
"There were," the emperor said, "no longer any Alps."

Time was all going was a mud hole rain or shine,
the motion of a hansom cab, a horse-drawn tram,
a tractor hauling omnibuses, a schedule, a line,
an elevated ride from the Battery to Courtland Street,
then uptown, five long miles, toward Central Park.
No black and yellow four-horse post-chaise,
no steam-powered coach from London out to Paddington,
no electric landaulet, no high-seat Dublin tricycle
made home so small, an anchorage of place,
as did the four-stroke engine under double cowls,
the hot-tube burner, and the chain-link drive.

Not long ago I stood beside a six-lane interstate;
behind me, in a field, the trace of an early road bed
cut toward Illinois, winding through the stubble;

the interstate ran full, with trailers, pick ups, vans.
A split-grill Bonneville sedan went by, as well,
a Toronado, a Cougar, and a Riviera coupe.
I saw all these, and more, wheels of every kind,
put motion in a still expanse, enlarging Indiana.

I raced once, a rebel in a custom Merc;
at other times, in Cadillacs and Continentals,
in Challengers and Firebirds, I cruised like a king;
in the Mission District in a dark green Fastback,
I easily outran the big-block Charger R/T at my back.
More often though, these days, I'm gridlocked,
trapped, in the afternoon, in a restless barreled eight;
or else, at night, with hairpin danger up ahead,
with foggy streets half-lit, no time to spare,
my two-toned Hudson Super Six will quit.

As exhausted foot-sore ploughmen trudged
(those patient walkers with their clouts and bags)
and shrine-bound wanderers on horseback went,
so on concrete highways, in a crush, all callings go.
Some eat the road, the holy line ahead of them,
in gas-lit voiturettes, in Zephyrs, long Minervas,
in Lagondas, Alfas, Wintons, Phantoms, Squires;
others, stuck in traffic, dream a burst of speed
while idling in Sting Rays, Mustangs, GTOs.
A few with choice of means by which to ride
insist, as they drive, that theirs is the right of way.
Take, for example, King Edward VII, in 1904,
out for a spin in his twenty-two horsepower Daimler.
The sudden prompt of a Gabriel Horn alerts us,
the deep carry of its three-note musical alarm,
and we find, if we want to live, the safety of a ditch,
as royalty speeds by, delighted with itself.

The Flagrant Dead

on the earliest photographic erotica

And here, too, are the libertines, the demi-reps,
of Finsbury Park and the Haymarket streets,
the gardens of pleasure in Cremorne and Soho,
with their gas-lit circles, crystal, and kiosks.
Reduced, long-dead, they incline, they awaken;
look, their earliest eyes, wide open, or seeming so,
from the bog-house, the cesspool, of sin,
stare back at us, demanding that we watch.

And in their eyes is the absolute suspension
of the pose, skirts lifted, knee socks down,
thick erection poised, its bold inaction held,
while an open shutter gathers in the light.
The women are supine or offer to be mounted,
staring back or up, and some with smiles,
while the men, their unbuttoned trousers
trenched below their thighs, shirt tails trailing,
heavy suspenders undone, lean forward,
toward and around the dark inviting center.
What strikes us most are the faces turned,
the looks of invitation in the dead immediate,
the easy letting go of all reserve.

Against this put pretense: nymphs and satyrs,
lovers on a swing or fleeing the sudden storm,
the moment when a dear intended paused,
her duty in the balance, to contemplate her heart.
Think, too, of how Rossetti made his wife
the "Blessed Beatrice" of his charged desire;
recall, as well, Alice's unbudded charm,
arranged just so, all pose, all likelihood.
Instead these images perform themselves;
these dead, like lunatics, avert no appetite;
their under-petticoats, their corded dimity
adorned like turkey-work, their pin-up coats
of Scotch plaid, tricked with bugle lace,
their gowns of printed calico, come off,
dead-level, down to this; no lace-trimmed
cambric shirt, no silk cravat, no beauty wash,

no essences of jasmine, keep all fresh,
in struggles long and hard against undress.

What anxious thought inhibits us tonight?
What dread of illness or of slouching gait?
Whose eyes are these, and whose attractive lips?
In mirrors, as we watch, our masks dissolve,
our glasses fill with spirited champagne;
we please ourselves to praise the flagrant dead,
to celebrate the vintage of their spending.

The Unveiling

Now the world's only
season's growing older,
the low stubble
of the shuttling sky
and night, too,
a blanket of conclusions.

Of course, we could also say:
when night comes,
whatever's in the ground
will keep like a new year
in winter's closet,
and, sooner or later, it, too,
will make ghosts of all
brief distinctions.

And add:
That these dead kin
are not so perfectly dead
as not to be somehow in motion,
somehow stored up in us,
their other limbs and faces,
here in the light.

But they were great
talkers once, themselves;
now they're as finished as the world is,
and done with listening, too.

What can we say about them,
having known them
as we cannot know the world?
What can we say about them now,
to keep them as kin?

Something should be said.
Now's the time to say something,
if we ever will,
about the differences
between love and the world.

David Bottoms

Under the Vulture-Tree

We have all seen them circling pastures,
have looked up from the mouth of a barn, a pine clearing,
the fences of our own backyards, and have stood
amazed by the one slow wing beat, the endless dihedral drift.
But I had never seen so many so close, hundreds,
every limb of the dead oak feathered black,

and I cut the engine, let the river gab the jon boat
and pull it toward the tree.
The black leaves shined, the pink fruit blossomed
red, ugly as a human heart.
Then, as I passed under their dream, I saw for the first time
its soft countenance, the raw fleshy jowls
wrinkled and generous, like the faces of the very old
who have grown to empathize with everything.

And I drifted away from them, slow, on the pull of the river,
reluctant, looking back at their roost,
calling them what I'd never called them, what they are,
those dwarfed transfiguring angels,
who flock to the side of the poisoned fox, the mud turtle
crushed on the shoulder of the road,
who pray over the leaf-graves of the anonymous lost,
with mercy enough to consume us all and give us wings.

The Desk

Under the fire escape, crouched, one knee in cinders,
I pulled the ball-peen hammer from my belt,
cracked a square of window pane,
the gummed latch, and swung the window,
crawled through that stone hole into the boiler room
of Canton Elementary School, once Canton High,
where my father served three extra years
as star halfback and sprinter.
Behind a flashlight's
cane of light, I climbed a staircase almost a ladder
and found a door. On the second nudge of my shoulder,
it broke into a hallway dark as history,
as whose end lay the classroom I had studied
over and over in the deep obsession of memory.

I swept that room with my light—an empty blackboard,
a metal table, a half-globe lying on the floor
like a punctured basketball—then followed
that beam across the rows of desks,
the various catalogs of lovers, the lists
of all those who would and would not do what,
until it stopped on the corner desk of the back row,
and I saw again, after many years the name
of my father, my name, carved deep into the oak top.

To gauge the depth I ran my finger across that scar,
and wondered at the dreams he must have lived
as his eyes ran back and forth
from the cinder yard below the window
to the empty practice field
to the blade of his pocket knife etching carefully
the long, angular lines of his name,
the dreams he must have laid out one behind another
like yard lines, in the dull, pre-practice afternoons
of geography and civics, before he ever dreamed
of Savo Sound or Guadalcanal.
                                        In honor of dreams
I sank to my knees on the smooth, oiled floor,
and stood my flashlight on its end.
Half the yellow circle lit the underedge of the desk,
the other threw a half-moon on the ceiling,
and in that split light I tapped the hammer

easy up the overhang of the desk top. Nothing gave
but the walls' sharp echo, so I swung again,
and again harder, and harder still in half anger
rising to anger at the stubborn joint, losing all fear
of my first crime against the city, the county,
the state, whatever government claimed dominion,
until I had hammered up in the ringing dark
a salvo of crossfire, and on a frantic recoil glanced
the flashlight, the classroom spinning black
as a coma.
              I've often pictured the face of the teacher
whose student first pointed to that topless desk,
the shock of a slow hand rising from the back row,
their eyes meeting over the question of absence.
I've wondered too if some low authority of the system
discovered that shattered window,
and finding no typewriters, no business machines,
no audiovisual gear missing, failed to account for it,
so let it pass as minor vandalism.
                       I've heard nothing.
And rarely do I fret when I see that oak scar leaning
against my basement wall, though I wonder what it means
to own my father's name.

A Chat with My Father

Sometimes when my old man tries to talk, his mind runs like a small boy
on a path through the woods.

You know the story. There's home to get to and it's getting late,
only a little light still slicing through the trees.

And the boy has walked the path so many times
he thinks he can do it in his sleep. But no. Some bird sounds off

way back in the woods, and he tries to ignore it, but it harps again,
and suddenly he's off the path, deeper and deeper

into the trees, wading the shadows, following the strangest
and most beautiful birdsong he's ever heard

until he crosses a stream and catches in the corner of his eye
a ruby as big as his fist, sure, a ruby or some rock

just as precious, and bends to pick it up when a wild dog . . .
no, not a dog, when a wolf barks across a gully,

and he's beating his way through brush and briar, trailing
those barks and howls already fading

in the distance. All the while the woods have grown dark,
and suddenly he looks across the table,

and you see in his eyes that he's lost.

J.O. Brachman

Lightning Bug Phenomenon

The males are the most light-flashing fireflies and appear in breath-taking elegance, flashing individually and, on occasions, in synchronized unison with literally thousands participating.
　　　　—The Encyclopedia Americana

Apostles of Luminous Impulses
night-flying in this dark,
dark sea of summer sky,
speak to me from humid depths
in a language of light.
Phosphorus-urged mates,
seen over there, there, now here.
But then a revolution begins,
as if a fiery tongue
descends upon the backyard,
organizes a chorus-flight,
no matter the location,
to blink on the same beat.
With my feet on the ground,
unfocused eyes open to the night,
I am alive, am possibly a tree,
the grass or one of the fireflies,
as if some mystery
about to be made clear,
tells me what needs to disappear.
And so I stop. My brain begins:
is it light-dark light-dark
or dark-light dark-light.
I miss the tempo of life,
cannot get it back.

Jesse Breite

Highway 40

An old red truck grumbles over
the dirt road's stiff heat. The trees lob
their branched weight to the West.
An empty beer can glistens sunshine.
A white-tailed hawk perches on a broken fence,
eyeing fat-lettuced fields of mouse and snake.
It's morning in Arkansas. Light spokes
through the plumed clouds. My father's head
rests on a white pillow. He dreams
of the old red truck, the empty beer can.
I watch the land unfold and disappear.
Arkansas is patiently inescapable.
The sharp-eyed king takes to flight—
from its needled claws, illegible shrieking.

Molly Brodak

Drawings of Ships

Some dimensions fall out of use,
out of the blue air, flat above you.

I didn't need to know that light is old.
There is always some broken net

caught in some cold cogs, not extraordinarily
silent, why fight? I fought because

I was so far off. Because I am in a kind
of love, sheer & oblique as depth-long seaweed.

Landscapes

No one's
here:

globe of branches,
movement of

small white
idiot insect

or mourning dove
crossing, squeaking

like a toy. Trees
eating sun. I can't

imagine
the white

hot back
of a crow

I caught
without trying

I caught
thinking I

could be time
in shining grass

Jody Brooks

Stealing Strawberries

Strawberry fields stretched between our neighborhood and the movie theater and after an action-packed matinee we couldn't resist. We lined up, one per row, the dirt paths like track lanes on the straightaway, the bottoms of our t-shirts held up like baskets. Mark, set, go. And we ran, grabbing fist-sized fruit, laughing and racing to the end as our shirt baskets filled. We grabbed the juiciest, the largest and firmest—we had to be quick as we scurried from plant to plant, always moving forward, secretly trying to beat each other to the end—while men in splintered wooden towers shot at us with pellet guns meant for rabbits. One of these men had grown tired of our racing game. He had seen us coming, climbed down from the tower and crouched behind a scrub brush on the far end of the field. When he caught Chelsea, she screamed. His hand clamped down on her arm and he pulled her t-shirt down, the ripe berries tumbling into dirt clods. The front of her exposed shirt was permanent-stained red like she'd been gut shot, like some strawberry sweet horror film. We ran to the end of the field and turned to watch, too scared to move, too proud to abandon our fruit. So we watched, one hand holding the bottoms of our t-shirts, the other shoving strawberry after strawberry to our dirty lips, tossing their green tops on the ground, never taking our eyes off our captured friend. We had no way of knowing what he hissed at her, his face too close, his spittle spraying her cheek. After a while he straightened up, lifted the pellet gun and pressed the barrel to her temple. He laughed and then lowered it, leaving a kiss mark on her pale skin.

Brian Brown

A Brief History of the Wiregrass

Your only business here is conjuring the past.

A tintype of your pioneer grandmother
is tattoed forever onto the one wall
left standing in the wake of the fire
that burned unnoticed, as a great-uncle
and obsolete cousins lay drunk in the fields,
helpless and shameless to the fate
of a doomed and all-too-simple architecture.

Your piedmont grandfather, asthmatic
orphan of the War Between the States,
settled here in 1912, among pocosins
rattling the threat of diamondbacks,
malarial hordes thick as a bible of plagues,
bound in a thorny leather
of prickly pear and palmetto.

This world born in the wink of a lightning storm,
born again and again, survives indifferent
to the extinction of its own place in history,
its sunstruck dogtrots screaming
at the blue velvet of midnight,
when clouds wave high over pines
like ghosts plundering time's emptiness.

One day you'll crucify yourself
on an old fencepost crowned with trumpet vine,
having sought your whole life a place here,
you'll attempt to change the storylines
in what's been a harsh folktale, and pray
the fire won't get anywhere near you,
until you've had time to really feel it,

crackling deep inside your bones.

Stacey Lynn Brown

Excerpts from Cradle Song: Sections I, II, and XXVII

I.

When I was four, we drove to Nashville,
Grand Ole Opry-bound, and stopped
the night at a broken down motel
in Tennessee—shag walls,
mossy carpet, dank concrete—
and I remember standing in
the doorway as evening fell,
a busful of believers rattling their way
to the pool for a makeshift
baptism, the *Amens* and *Hear us, Lords*
ricocheting through the courtyard
as underwater lights glowed
the pool algae green.

They would come to him, the big
preacher man, and he'd lay
a palm across their foreheads, brace
them at the small of their backs.
They'd release themselves to him:
teethsucking the air before
falling back into salvation,
held under unstruggling and
splashing up anew all gasping
grace and sanctified glory
hallelujah til my mother shut the door
and made me watch tv.

My parents don't recall it,
but that's the way
memory works in the South—
the truth is always lying
in some field somewhere between
the bones of the fallen
and the weapons they reach for.

II.

Down South, all it takes
to be a church are some stencils
and a van. And my childhood
was full of them:

The Episcopal litanies of Sunday school
exercises in genuflection,
the low country Southern Baptist pit
of hellfire and damnation

hemming us inside the tent
while just outside,
flies hoverbuzzed above
plattered chicken, slaw, and beans.

Prophets profiteering in spoken
tongues as the Charismatic
wailed and thrashed and shook
their Babel babble down.

In dirt-floored shacks, fevered
believers danced themselves
into a frenzy, coiling snakes like copper
bracelets dangling from their wrists,

spit-cracked lips and boot heel clog,
the bass line itself almost enough
to give you back your faith.
Grape juice in Dixie

cups, cardboard host, backwashed
wine, this grit who'd been told
to be still and learn
was never any closer to God

than when I stood at the back of that
whitewashed clapboard A.M.E. I could only
ever visit: The preacher pacing the worn
strip of rug, pleading, *Help us, Lord,*

teach us how to love,
sending testified ripples that washed
over heads nodding bobs
on the waves of his words:

choir rocking, feet stomping, peace
only to be found in the swing skirt of shimmy
and the big-bellied voices booming it holy
in the gospel of *move and know* sway.

XXVII.

My grandfather who, in his day, had been tyrant, holy, keeper of the gothic
ornaments of religion, strict, penitent, and unlistening, obstinate slammer of
        doors
and disavowing thief of family, was, in the end, reduced in that diapering
        inevitability
to velcro shoes and sweatshirts with his name sewn in the collar.
Through the halls of the hollerers he ambled his walker, navigating the
        squeaky labyrinth
of disease, despair, and dementia, down to the Medicare wing, his picture on
        the door
to guide him to the right bed beside an endless stream of roommates
        reaching their ends,
their messy living and dying scrubbed down, then freshly sheeted.

My grandfather, who, in his day, painted landscapes so beautiful I wanted
to live inside them, sang baritone and bass gospel on revival chitlin circuits,
taught classes in foot care for sciatic-sore millworkers, and bagged groceries at
        the Bi-Lo after car and child collided, was, in the end,
only able to remember fits and starts of *Amazing Grace.*
Through four nursing homes he listed aimlessly, building model Fords from
        popsicle sticks,
singing fragments of redemption songs, his vast immobility childing him
        small and sunken
like the furthest flung stone against a glass house of dying, lobbed up and
        heavied back
down again to the room where I would sit, holding his absence, his paper-
        thin hand.

Kathryn Stripling Byer

Coastal Plain

The only clouds
forming are crow clouds,

the only shade, oaks
bound together in a tangle of oak

limbs that signal the wind
coming, if there is any wind

stroking the flat
fields, the flat

swatch of corn.
Far as anyone's eye can see, corn's

dying under the sky
that repeats itself either as sky

or as water
that won't remain water

for long on the highway: its shimmer
is merely the shimmer

of one more illusion that yields
to our crossing as we ourselves yield

to our lives, to the roots
of our landscape. Pull up the roots

and what do we see but the night
soil of dream, the night

soil of what we call
home. Home that calls

and calls
and calls.

Scuppernongs

They ripened to myth on her tongue, sweetness
always beyond reach, out there at the edge
of abandoned farms, back in the thickets
where no decent woman dared go. Not that she
scorned the mayhaws her black neighbors left
at her door. Toiling hours in tropical swelter,
she boiled them down into a red syrup

salvaged in jelly jars. How much of her sweat
she stirred into that crimson stock I still
contemplate when it comes time to make jelly
again and I find myself roaming the fruit stalls
till I smell them, lifting both hands full,
as she would have done, to my nose,
understanding why she bent to every plum,

melon, and peach, every strip of fresh sugar cane.
Thus have these scuppernongs ripened
for too long inside my refrigerator.
Past time to ward off the coming rot,
time to remember how she'd set to work
with no recourse to Sure-Gel. Just lemon and
sugar. A spoon. Cheesecloth. Most of a morning

or afternoon, watching the syrup drip slowly,
then more slowly still down the spoon's sticky
edge. Leaving everything it touched, as always,
a mess, and for what? On my windowsill,
seven jars through which the light of this late
summer afternoon takes its time, quickening
each pot of pale amber juices to sweet everlasting.

Gone Again

I used to believe Scarlett would forever be
     standing atop that small rise of Georgia clay
staring at Tara, intoning Tomorrow, Tomorrow,
     that sad pace of syllables, the Old South
newly colorized, ready to hoodwink another generation
     of belles. But I won't be among them,
no doddering old lady still telling of how
     I remember my mother reciting her tales
of the premiere at Loew's, all Atlanta agape
     at the glitterati. No ma'am,

I have sat through that gorgeous monstrosity
     five times in English and once in dubbed
Spanish. Miss Scarlett does not anymore stir
     me into a passion of Southernness.

Once I imagined myself limping home
     with a worthless mule, nothing but rags
in a wagon, waiting for the moon to reveal
     the house still standing, me weeping
into my muddy hands, having survived
     such a journey and all for a lost cause.

I didn't much like Scarlett after the war.
     Standing there in the moonlight
was our shining moment, unfazed by
     the real sounds of hound dogs
     and katydids, down on the road
a horn playing Dixie, its drunk driver heading
     back home to his fraternity house.
          So frankly, my dear,

I don't give a damn whether or not Scarlett's
     barbecue ball gown looks brand new
          after 62 years. Scarlett makes me feel
tired—all those hours I wasted, enraptured
     by someone whose skin was pure
celluloid, whose voice, when the reel came
     loose, gibbered like mine when I tried
to pretend I lived just down the road
     from that movie set, cotton fields painted
          on canvas, the loyal slaves hoisting
               up sacks full of nothing
          but chaff for the wind, that old
     Hollywood hack, to keep blowing away.

Melisa Cahnmann-Taylor

Goldkist Poultry, Athens, Georgia

So cold it could be Alaska on the plant floor
where body heat, endurance, and speed

shelter those with same social security names,
same blue hairnets and gloves. They've moved

from Huehuetenango to Georgia and Texas,
smuggled with them *pupusas* and *discotecas*.

They're indentured to where Leonel can make $7.75
to slice chicken legs: wage enough for a small *piñata*,

a quarter tank of gas. I came South to teach
poetry but the guidance counselor misheard me, reached

a hand to where the wind blows, said the smell
first strikes the throat. *Poetry* and *po' try*, neither one

exact science to measure what's good or done.
So I decided to tour the plant

to learn how families worked while I hurled
children to defiance in verse.

I hoped they'd use words
like *feathers in flight over mud*,

not *shackled* or *smocked* in couplets of *blood*.

In the Name of God

I don't care for a bearded God
who throws spit or stones.
You can keep your spilled blood,
your wrestlers and victors. I want
a God who sweats when she dances,
who craves dark chocolate, a God
of multitudes who plays H.O.R.S.E..
I want One who listens, a yogi
who moves from plank pose to upward
facing dog. I want a vegan God
who eats bacon, One without judgment,
who's patient and knits sweaters,
who isn't afraid to change his mind.
God, almighty King of the Universe—
I don't want *that* chauvinistic bully
to forgive me. I don't care for robes
or loincloths, velvet or cashmere or
whose God has the better basketball team.
The One I love is not yours, not mine,
not so easily possessed, not a God who owns
property or wears vests full of explosives.
Your God leaves a funny taste in my mouth.
The One who has a rich feast in the foyer
of a finer structure or sings in the sweeter sorrow
of a minor key—all these Gods, the male
and female, the dead and the risen,
keep them, call them whatever you like.
I want a God whose name is all names,
whose enemies are arrogance and war,
whose peace is as present as the purple crocus'
possible bloom in spring.

Brent Calderwood

Nocturne

Perhaps it is better to wake up after all, even to suffer,
rather than to remain a dupe to illusions all one's life.
—Kate Chopin, The Awakening

In dreams, you read my poems, I'm never in bed
past noon, no one snores. I still cook the same
four meals in the Teflon pan. You bake banana bread
drenched in butter, sear pink cubes of tuna, steam
asparagus. A ceramic lamp on your nightstand glows
pink, green, then so smoothly to blue the change
is barely apparent. We drool on the same pillows
for two more years. But aside from my limited range
at the stove, nothing's based in fact. It's fiction,
like the only novel we'd both read, about a flawed
hero who wants more than a well-larded kitchen.
Last night, you wore a hand-lettered sandwich board,
bits of dialogue snatched from the book: *because I*
love you—and on the back, you'd written *Goodbye*.

Rain

Here comes the rain again.
The tsunami came to Japan yesterday
and five thousand miles to the east,
the bay is huge, swaying and gray,
an elephant butting its head into the dunes.
When the plovers come back tomorrow,
they'll perforate the sand in neat little rows,
searching for whatever it is plovers eat.

I want to walk in the open wind.
But it's coming so hard I have to hold
my umbrella like a riot shield,
the metal legs straining in the squall.
I should pick up a phone. I should call
my sister-in-law. She lost her husband on Friday.
I should call my mother, who lost one of her sons
but who does that anymore—pick up a phone, I mean?
We carry them with us.

I want to talk like lovers do.
The night of the election
I was missing your big kitchen,
the seasoned pan, that trick you taught me
for cutting onions. The next morning
it was like the poster said, HOPE—
I even thought of calling you,
even forgot about the marriage amendment.
My family didn't—think to call, I mean.
No one said "We can't believe it lost."

I want to dive into your ocean.
In the video, Annie Lennox
is walking into the sea like Virginia Woolf,
or, if that was a river, then like James Mason
at the end of A *Star is Born*—the good version.
MTV wouldn't play her at first—
Annie Lennox, I mean—
they said she looked too much like a man.

Is it raining with you?
Last week I saw a seal pup wash onto the shore,
a black purse spilling open with opals, rubies,
so fresh the gulls hadn't found it yet—
they were still squawking downwind
round a crab, and when I came close they flew off.
Their feet had scratched out a wreath of little V's,
three rows deep, each pointing out from the middle,
away from the ticking thing,
half-eaten, half-alive.

Kevin Cantwell

The Next Abstinence

Tonight, hold that white pill between your teeth—careful
not to place your tongue to it, that first Percocet bitten
    like a cube of sugar some will pour their black tea around.
Let the jar of water wait to be sipped. Let the night lawn whiten with frost.
    Refrain tonight from all you lack. Consider how to do without
another bite—not the pink ribs of a suckling shoat picked to strips;
    nor the last nibbled flesh of a Winesap left so scarce at its core
that the nautilus of its lucent membrane windows the seeds.

    Let the last cigarette grow stale; let your memory of it
sweeten. And still gripping that painkiller, bite down to make it half.
    So, if not tonight, & not at once, soon at least, your needs
will grow less incessant of their easy clams: this one tablet, split
    in two, will take you to that one gray hour that is not yet day;
& so, put off the peace it will bring you. Later, take that second half
    at dusk. Break it into twos & those halves then into quarters;
& broken—break *them*, until what you have is a kind of dust
    & then nothing but the stars on sleepless nights
& the moon—

full & then its half.

Night Game Vexed by a Line from Melville

Moth-time, midsummer, the bedroom in the dark.
>For a while out west in Oakland, the blue lid of twilight

fluttered over the stadium like the milk eye of the world
>putting off sleep. For a moment the game was a base-hit

from done. Now, too lonely to stand, a few fans
>wait out the extra-innings into the early morning—

the length of a night-shift & then never going home.
>In the breath it would take to unfold the fan of a newspaper,

the centerfielder turns to go back for something.
>Even on the radio I can hear him call for it

in that shell of sleep—& Melville himself, restless
>with the voices on the wind, a crowd & its *mixed surf*

of *muffled sound* from his house-top room—
>the draft riot in Lower Manhattan late in the war.

One of Those Russian Novels

Sumatra, Florida

On a chalk road north of Sumatra,
we drove inland from the ocean's light.
The leaves were paper; rain, the gray light
of stars on a white-grass river.

We drove inland from the ocean's light;
we drove from the flat sea, past a house—
past rain-stars on a white-grass river,
the house set back in tents of hemlock.

We drove from the gray sea, past a house
run with water streaks, two stories up,
set back in rain, in tents of hemlock
& stands of palmetto, stands of pine.

Run with droops of moss, two stories up,
as in one of those Russian novels,
but here in palmetto; here, in pine—
a house, a room, a man by himself.

As in one of those Russian novels,
but here—eating his chocolate cake,
a room at dusk, a man by himself
whose son will not come to the table.

Here, a man eating chocolate cake,
on his son's birthday, whose mother weeps,
& who will not come to the table,
who sits on a couch in the ruined trees.

On his birthday the boy's mother weeps
& hears rain & a car going by,
& sits on a couch in the ruined trees
& hears a man weep at a table,

who hears the rain, a car going by
through paper leaves, rain made of gray light—
& hears himself weep at a table
near a chalk road north of Sumatra.

Michelle Castleberry

A Man's World, 1966

"Hair and teeth. A man got those two things he's got it all."
–James Brown

The woman just out of the frame
could be adjusting a wreath or crown
from the way your eyes roll up
under the weight of some blessing
or coronation, some syncopated call.
"Good God!"

Instead, your attendant takes out
a series of yellow and pink hair curlers
before shaping that righteous bouffant.
The broad Apache cheekbones cup the light
and your face tilts like a saint's.

The dark spindrift of hair and full mouth,
the heavy torso of a kouros under the Japanese robe.
"I don't know karate but I know cuh-razy!"
It takes a lot of man to be this pretty.

Not yet the white noise of the crowd,
not yet the hot lights or the banshee cries
that come from a place
not even you recognize.
There's still time to hear the sound of
a theater holding its breath,
the popgun snap
of chairs folded shut and stacked,
cramped wallflowers shunned
off the still drumhead of the floor.

Until then, your dresser breathes and hums
around the bobby pins in her mouth.
She is barely heard
over the phantom music
of the set list in your head.
You run the changes
and tumble the songs
like dominos, like dice, like coins.

Bounty

The pickled wind off the pond
made our eyes water,
our noses run and redden.
His face bled out to the color
of the fish bellies that coated
the water like dull sequins.
He never retched
but walked stiff,
each movement a remainder
of the effort to stay upright.

Daddy coughed out numbers,
from each silver hatchling
to gas money for the drive to Fordyce,
then toted the cost against
the unmade sums for filets,
whole fish, and scraps
sold to trappers.

He continued his
arithmetic of loss
while a crane near the levee
dipped like an oil rig
to binge and get sick,
binge again on the bounty.

Katie Chaple

Pretty Little Rooms

—*The remains of who was thought to be the Renaissance poet Francesco Petrarch are instead those of two different people, DNA tests have confirmed.*

The skull was unexpected, a surprise in the pink marble tomb.
In 1873, the old doctor of Padua claimed it had crumbled,
as though too injured to live outside that stone room.
Did he keep it on his desk? On his shelf as a specimen,
an exemplar of perfection, the knitted plates
a symbol of all that we cannot know of love?

The doctor was not the only man who needed—a friar fled
his flagged cell, hacked off the poet's arm, spirited it back,
a drunk friar in such grief for the world, so moved
as to steal the physical. And where and how to keep it—
this limb that had once moved to love's measure?

And now, these scientists with their test tubes, their milliliters
and tweezers are used to wounds and hairs, blood
and shatter. In their white coats and labs, they don't ask
questions they don't know the answers to. They brush
away quarry dust, measure the circumference, count the alleles,
and approximate the years—all equating female.
Nobody asks: Whose body was not loved enough
that her skull could travel like a pebble,
could be used to punctuate the line of a man's body?

Gross Anatomy

My cousin tells me about his cadaver, Baby,
as we pass the lab where she lies.
Says that by the second session, he was stripping
the husk of skin, slitting Baby's chest,
cracking the ribs, flipping them open
like the lapels of a vest, to expose that network,
a skein of threads weaving muscles.
He tells me about the mass of wires,
that you tell an artery from a vein by the snap
of it breaking in two like a hair.

The week they work on Baby's head,
his study group goes for gin fizzes on the river front,
a bar with scarred stools and tattooed necks,
straight bones of pool cues and sharp glint of belt buckles.
He's checking out this girl—
her soft slope from neck to collarbone—
and is thinking about how to strike up talk,
how to work in that he is a med student,
when he has a vision of himself
lifting off Baby's face like the lid of a box,
seeing the fullness of eyes. Then, stark white—
the mandible, a bone that cleans up so nicely—
against red cheek muscles.
He sees the loops of tendons bridging
wider, then narrowing to the next bone.

Shaking his head, he sees under everyone's face,
everyone's the same—bartender, couple kissing in the corner,
hanging on, touching each other only with their mouths,
the man with his hand in his pocket, who's been eyeing
the door all night. He knows that it only takes a drag of the knife
to uncover the whole bar. That couple.
He remembers pinching her chin,
pressing closed the gap
between jaws, teeth to bone.

Elizabeth J. Colen

Little Bird

Winter. Daddy in the war. Only mother's blood. Only in the pale pink kitchen, the winter sky of knife. Five. Daddy paid the price. Head in oven, head over head tumble down the stairs. Sky. She never learned how in the pink she becomes dislodged. There's a secret here. We're in it. There were two of you. The Hummer breaks. Beat box. They came for you. Summer waits inside. Stutter. Neighbor's blonde brick wall cultivates wicked snakes of ivy. Ivy wrecks the plaster. Three drops of blood seep through savage suburban dream. Mother watched the wall. Heard the call. Blades destroying sound and thought. The blood. Carrot carnage, sway of milk, rubbed out ivory, ivory love, black helicopter. Generosity of courage or forgetfulness, nothing remains but fog. Then a tree full of red that emerges when blackened noise begins to clear.

Stephen Corey

Abjuring Political Poetry

Some men will shoot an infant in the face.
There, that's a start—near pentameter, even.
Has the world been bettered yet, or your mood?

The only mirror of horror is itself.
Art's a game when it thinks it shows the world
in actuality; art's a savior
when it stalks the world as art: stone as stone,
paint as paint, words as the music of words.

Here's a joke we children laughed at once:
What's the difference between a truckload
of bowling balls and one of dead babies?
You can't unload the balls with a pitchfork.

It's okay to laugh—that shows you sense the awfulness.
Imagine the hearer who did not get the joke:
No poem could reach him. No horror. No world.

Emily Dickinson Considers Basketball

In breathing—air is foremost still—
No perfect set of lungs
Makes headway in a vacuum—
Nor sings uncharted songs—

And yet the map is viable
according to its lands—
on fingertips the whorlings
explain the hearts of hands—

And so this child—in alleyways—
perfects his picks and shots—
while that one—God's own spotlight takes
to blare his body's cuts.

But both—give me the language—
to speak their passion's moves
as if the fact of motion
made horses—talk with hooves—

Or angels sing with flutterings
their tongues need not support—
the round and up and in and out—
sufficient proof of art—

Universe

The one turning is all we seek:
a warm noon breeze at winter's end,
the child's fever breaking in time,
the single pair of eyes our way
in the overcrowded room—
their depth-gaze proclaiming
we are, beyond all doubt,
the one. Turning is all we seek:
butter from milk, hawk in gyre,
leaf in whirlpool, steel from fire,
many strong backs against violence and war,
old prejudice into respect for
the one turning. Is all we seek
a shift from sameness, the grave's precursor
Poe saw daily in his canted mirror?
Or do we wish for change like God's, all
revolving and evolving within the great bubble
the one turning is? All we seek
drives us to question the sought—
what worth this canvas daubed with paint,
this debit to the ledger, this rush of blood
in bed or birth or slaughter?
How long can we move ourselves to believe
the one turning is all? We seek
the change that does not mean the end—
aloneness into love, dullness to arousal,
flat brown fields to gauze of sprouting green—
the change that primes and perks us
for the world, mutes the narrow notion
the one turning is all we. Seek
and ye shall seek—there's a turn
that turns a phrase our way.
We have pancakes and pirouettes,
Satan's anus-gate to heaven,
hot to cold, elation to despair,
rock to lava to rock.
We have the child's first smile, first step, first word.
And everywhere we look we look, and
the one turning is all we seek.

Daniel Corrie

World's Time

Familiar, transient . . . .
    −Marcus Aurelius

I dream a quiet moccasin cuts its path
on a shimmering surface. New apples gleam
in the orchard I remember. The horizon's seam
glimmers, a thread's line stitched through cloth
whose pattern bleaches out in sunlight. The smell
of mown grass turns to sleep. The sun centers,
providing sky the meaning of noon. A canna enters
into summer, becoming the color of its spell.

Then I dream the evening purples. Dusk runs out,
closing to some other space. Some unreachable recess
lies past the field where a tireless tractor plows
the unremembering earth. In twilight's fall, the flash
of birdcall shelters silence. The evening finally glows
into the dusk of hours, accepting everything at last.

The Years

. . . the flow of time we call history . . . .
–Barry Lopez

Then soldiers in gray stopped their file.
From the cellar of the shack they lugged
blocks of ice they stacked on rigs.
The white woman and black children stood,

gazing after the men, carts, and horses
rounding the dirt road's curve, into summer.
Then the roof is fallen as the snow
melts dripping from the joists.

A caved in hut, the elm. At forest's edge
five muddy goats appear. Bending low
their twisted horns, they yank at sedge.
Eyes of gold. Then the rustle of

the others, shades trudging up
the hill at dusk, bandaged and beggarish.
They pitch their rifles in the snow.
One glances up as though startled

by a mirror hung in a stranger's home
he'd entered to loot. His eyes close.
He breathes his prayer for those who will
finally make it past an open field

or who will meet themselves in crossing
like the junco as it jolts against
its own image in the window glass.
A gaze was dazed, smoke-stung, glimpsing

a final shape of elm, branching past seeing.
Rain healed the dirt road of the wounds
of the tracks of wagon wheels and horses.
Fifteen decades died to days and nights.

The goats file on to the shabby pen
to rut and mingle in the night.
The old stump rots, rising, elm opening
arms of madonna, her branches offering.

Money

Money is time given permanent form—
though of course only for a time.
             —Howard Nemerov

The backs of dollars open in
the green inscriptions. A dollar's center
opens, a window of white space.

The window looks toward some distant
destination, some destiny
beyond the laurels of green ink.

It is a distance never to be
manifest. The whiteness of snow
descends into the vista of snow,

oblivion's cartography.
The blankness at the dollar's center
becomes the ground of every wish.

In the dollar's field of emptiness,
the green ink colonizes to
a figure. Its contour's capitals

inscribe the great, green ONE.
It boldly dawns, like meaning's shape
imprinted on the void of white.

The bill's four corners echo it
ONE ONE ONE ONE
tolling a plural loneliness

of each divided, as each is swept
separately to separate corners.
One by one, hand by hand,

nations of hands reach out to grip.
Turning and turning in cyclonic
swirls of fingerprints, all dollars

will gust from hands, funneling higher
in circuits of the ancient winds
intent to own all human keepsakes.

70

Like a world burst into bees,
bills swarm and veer into a blur
of fortune's humming, churning cloud.

As bills reverse, they turn their edges
to disappear, then ripple into
human faces. Enshrined in ink,

Washington meets the viewer's gaze.
Hamilton and Jackson stare
away, past crests and troughs of values.

Their solemn faces drift in fame
as though across small movie screens.
Like single, frozen frames from movies,

they act their roles beyond their deaths.
They pose in postures of permanence,
forever in their paper countries.

Hand after hand folds and unfolds
currencies tarnishing in commerce,
soiling with oil of hand after hand.

The spectral smudge of every touch
is left behind, faint evidence
of spending's ghosts, of endless costs.

Once upon a dime's bright time,
a miser hoarded treasure, till
he'd emptied all of his time's tills.

Once pawned, a time can never be
redeemed. Rich dreams of futures steal
untils. Years roll away, like pennies.

Chad Davidson

Target

Dear Arrowhead water, dear feather boa, dear father
and mother with the toddler and cartful of candles:

I wanted to tell you the sky swished open its doors
this morning, the whole shebang slid by on felt,

and I entered the mythic fires of stoicism,
bore my nakedness in the manner of Shackleton,

defiantly ignorant. For I know that Target, centerless
like new pedagogies, loves the good good,

loves punishment somehow instructing
a niche audience. That's me. I love to finger

the Milano-style whatnot, bend the necks
of five-headed floor lamps. Yes, I love you dearly,

dear church of the cherished storage bin,
dear Cheerios and the bowl to drown you in,

dear warehouse sky, dear reindeer aiming the beads
of your eyes at my impulse buys. Once, I shot a gun

in the desert, laid it down in the sand, and said
a small prayer to prayers of small sizes.

Years later, we navigated the marked-downs
and Doritos safe in their Mylar pillows,

thought we'd stripped ourselves clean
of desire's burrs and foxtails, even as popcorn

promised low-sodium transubstantiation.
We were *registering*, the word itself green and bearded,

so aimed our fantastic machines at the crock
pot and bath rug, at the iPod snug in its skin.

We dressed ourselves in the warmth of that small space
heater, fed the nuisance of class consciousness

little biscuits. How cloudless, how terrible and lucid
the distances we traveled for our dear wedding guests—

dear, which my Italian friend uses in that foreign way,
as in, *That pair of pants is too dear*. And how dear, how shear

the night, we thought, dearly beloved, outside the Target,
the headlights of all those cars trained on us.

Cleopatra's Bra

It is one thing to uphold one's passions,
another to retain them. That thin seam
between impassioned and fashion: it could be

just another form of governing,
intimacy. Who knows if sequins spiraled
around each nipple, lapis clinging to straps.

Each mouthful of wine would raise her body heat
until a touch of gold slivered and rose
off her dark skin, caught somewhere

in a jewel of sweat. This is the Egypt
I imagine: pyramids, obelisks,
the Valley of Kings, and one torn bra.

Meanwhile, the Romans fashioned their parchment,
filled it with long strings of letters: *a*
for *ave*, *b* for *beato* (blessed), *c*,

of course, for *Caesar*, with no space between,
as to appear infinite. Augustus did try.
The old argument: *come home, she's bad news*.

But for Antony there would be no empire
cloven: a pregnant dream as he lay
again with her, clothes strewn on the ground

like artifacts of a forgotten city
under ash, and those two bodies caught
once more, together, for all of Rome to see.

Because it did end, Virgil says, in ruins
of a city, toppled towers, and one
fictitious Dido who let it all hang out

one Carthage summer so hot the oarsmen
gave up their fears, Acestes descended his throne
without bearskin, Aeneas loved and left,

Dido died. I like to imagine her scrawling
a message to the future regarding love—
flagrant love—and sacrificial fires

like those she clothed her city in one night:
Beware the Roman come to lie with you,
one hand heart-heavy and bound there

like the swearing-in of a city
official. Feeling her lover fiddle
with the clasp, Cleopatra must have thought,

does everything come undone with this
one small breach of virtue? One giant step
backward, she hears the inevitable

unleashing of the dogs, the centuries
head to toe in armor, and the lift,
they say, of a shallow wicker basket.

I like to imagine her calmly spreading
her robe, a leisurely cup of wine,
her fingers unclasping the bra from behind

as the asp negotiates the sea
of azure silk that separates them, empires
colliding, and the golden tint of scales.

Ginkgo

Shit stones, crap berries, barf balls, the stink
not of death but of the dying, the bedsores
festering in little lakes of purple: none of this
I knew the winter we hauled into our first house

the fruits of our lives together—cat-scratched
couch, a few wobbly bookshelves, slender legs
of a table we sanded and stained and were proud of.
The tree, you see, offered nothing as obscene.

Embarrassingly bare, its thin branches clattered
against February, in a host of ghostly winds
summoned by some silver-haired god in love
with nothing but the bliss of not knowing,

not smelling. For the Ginkgo, *silver apricot* of Japan,
conjures a stench ineffable enough to frighten atheists
back into the dense foliage of faith, its linger cruel
as a joke—not the *ha-ha* kind but the stab, the taunt

of the bully, the dog shit in the flame of a paper bag.
Neither did it puke forth that first summer, or second,
when, in a bout of possession, I hacked a limb
crowding the power lines. And when the orange men

arrived for the briar and beheld the maimed Ginkgo
all horror and poised in the manner of an ideograph
shorn of political significance, when the taller one
with fewer stains asked with no small stone

of outrage in his mouth, *What kind of monster
does that to a Ginkgo?* I only shook my head
and muttered the name of the previous owner.
And why not, since the Ginkgo, you know,

is a survivor, it and the cockroaches the first
to return to the radiated thoroughfares
of Hiroshima and Nagasaki? This is true.
I read it in the signature of Florence Norton,

wife of Claude, the woman who signed us over
this house and Ginkgo. Because it's the precision
with which we forget, the technology of it all,
that's most frightening. That's what I imagine

Florence must have thought when she drove by
months after the deal, beheld what we did
to her yard stripped of its pines, the rash of azaleas
systematically erased, the Ginkgo's amputation.

Frightening, which, when read in the lilt
of her notecard's decorum sent to us days later,
came across as *lovely*, what we had done, she said,
lovely as the Ginkgo immortalized by Li Shanji

at the temple of Qingcheng, just a name
that means *Lush Thicket Mountain*, birth place,
it turns out, of the very first Ginkgos,
some of the oldest living things on this peach pit,

I shit you not, none of which helps me now
as the crap berries fall again, their vomitous reek
carried in on the paws of the cat, the wheels of the car,
the address of the dead, whose mail still arrives.

I've read where you can graft a male branch
and thus Tiresias-like toggle the sex, shut down
the fruit. Others counsel going on a sacred search
for some mythic Chinese mystics who'd leap

at the chance to collect free Ginkgo fruit
for poultices and memory aids, which sounds good,
since I'd like the opposite: to forget it all,
and watch, out this window—whose sill is still

cemented by paint from Florence and Claude—
the women in wide hats arrive by mule caravan,
spread their tarps below this Ginkgo, disdain its wound,
and shake the branches for all they're worth.

Travis Denton

The Burden of Speech

How inept the first man and woman
must have found themselves, striving toward utterance.
Og grunting as he painted stick figures and buffalo outlines
in charred coals or deer blood on the cave walls,
apparently in answer to
                    Honey, what did you do today?

And after learning to bang syllable into word
like arrows from rock,
he must have been troubled to know he learned to speak
only to repeat endlessly—*That's not what I meant*—.
Did he wish he could leave behind all those labials and fricatives
that he carried on his back like a knapsack and bow?

And later, much later, after glaciers began their trek back
north or south, screeching past bedroom windows,
smashing the occasional hut,
leaving only a soggy marsh in their wake
everyone learned to say *telephone*,
and put away their kindling and flint.

Then, with the days of rummaging grassy plains
or spearing sunfish in the village stream well behind him,
the only record of his former self
frozen in history books like family albums—
his photo captioned:
Og hunts berries for his clan,
he found himself at the foot of some babbling tower,
leather briefcase in one hand, soy latte in the other,
voices dripping like honey down the marble and glass walls,
puddling into a bog and leaving him standing
like a fountain in the center,
spitting phonemes and vowels,
"to be" verbs clicking from his pockets
and disappearing in the mire.
But alas, encumbered by the deadweight of words,
our hero sinks, too tired to call to those on the bank for a line,
but clawing at his jacket pockets for his cell.

Local Men

They're the ones you read about in the papers,
Never good news. For Example: *Local Man, Found Face Down
In His Teriyaki at Bill's Lucky Buddha, Foul Play Suspected.*
Look around, gaggles of local men,
Just waiting to be picked off—thrown in the back
Of a rusted-out Buick (said car last seen speeding
Away from the Circle K). Hog-tied, drugged, stripped,
And left on Main Street. Local men aimed
For blunt force trauma of all kinds—you name it,
A 2x4 will do the job, candelabra, a length of iron pipe.

Wrong turns, blown red lights, each turn of the key
Has hurried them here, yet they appear surprised
When the strange car pulls up beside them
As they exit the wash-o-mat.
Their checkered pasts, like a one-legged runner, laps them.
They are lost wallets, keys that just go missing—lives
Summed up in two inches of newsprint.
They are not the last of the Mohicans.
Not the last dodo to lie down somewhere on the back forty.
But, a brown coat, scuffed shoes, a partial thumbprint,
A moustache sitting on a bar stool
In a local bar, who none of the other locals notice
Until the cops show up with photo asking,
Have you seen this man?

Michael Diebert

Dream Songs: Summer, Atlanta

1

Ninety. Unbudging air. Fans roar
in sync with my boiling body.
Mr. Meteorology,
when will your point-n-clicker click
to a screen other than bleak
unbroken warm fronts? Anymore

kudzu's done scaled the treetops
and's building a railway to the ozone.
Forecast that, rain freak!
Slight chance of storms. Yawn. Bring a book.
The single unstealable thing of mine:
mind and its overheated hops

in this hothouse hotter in than out.
It was ninety-two.
Heaven would be a bathtub of ice
in an air-conditioned car. Or right about.
As for you,
Mr. Man, no squall can save your face.

2

Huffy Henry's harried half-grandnephew Hunter
beheld the garage freshly swept
and the absence of the family feline—
freshly swept, he surmised, into clothes hamper
or carted off to vet,
dead they said by any reckoning.

Twelveheartedly Hunter jammed
the needle into the lately
little-used basketball, pumped much air,
went outside, threw up greatly

from three-point land innumerable prayers,
wholly, immeasurably bummed—

safe to say, we'll say, he made it a mission,
force-fed that ol' albatross.
By noon, closure also dead.
Viva layup of chaos!
Viva hook shot of confusion!
But man oh man was he twelveheartedly sweaty and red.

7

East bound and down, Snowman out. Son!
If they only knew . . .
You had to kneel before Elvis's throne,
finger-pick your way back through
the horns and strings and things. What next?
Of course! Swamp redneck!

True, your wily wiseass side was the best.
But the ballads! Near-torch songs,
confessions: you were mushy and sincere.
Full out, boys—Personaville or bust!
To reprobates and lovers both you sang.
We never caught up. You'd long kicked it in gear.

When you're hot, you're hot, and you were, there, for a while.
Upon your passing, something else has passed—
scratchy, gutbucket holler
of a field rat/faith healer,
of a fervent hermit at loudmouthed peace
with the two-faced, knife-wielding world.

—Jerry Reed, 1937-2008

11

Flies drove spikes into our thighs
the very last time the family camped.
South Carolina, July.
We were made snippy and awfully proud.
Switch on the radio, strip down, jump
in the lukewarm lake, hide.

That is, endure.
The Coleman hissed its blue fire.
Sleepless, Dad made up impossible machines,
bigger and friendlier fish.
We burned for separate rooms, for monsoons.
Tradition a sudden unexplainable rash.

Love, please forgive me when I rail against the heat,
at night fling off all possible bedsheets.
Actually I'm smiling.
Why through this season persevere?
One, you're here.
Two, to pass from pique into a season of healing.

12

Aesthete, here's your Olympian pool and your soft-focused summer.
Here's your weathered chaise and your paper-encased burger,
and here's your bikinied teen angel.
Here's your lifeguard with his Olympian whistle—
okay, okay, and your pale befuddled parents.
Plenty of paint. Don't be scared.

Even though it was overcast, I'm making it blue,
and I won't fill in many other people . . .
Now hold on a cotton-pickin' minute!
I never said I wanted anything in it!
But maybe a dab of purple
there at the margin behind the domed barbecue

and somewhere a daffodil,
and the mood of the thing would be nice to see,
what Dad's wrinkled brow perhaps really means . . .
Okay. You want me to paint an entrance
to a boarded-up building. Yes. Well,
friend, now you've not a painting but a séance.

Maudelle Driskell

The Propaganda of Memory

You stand in the picture, all khaki and gleam,
where the sun found you grinning
around the stump of a cigar, holding
a wooden friar ransacked
from a French churchyard.
In the field of smoke-banked light behind you,
in the rubble of gas masks, and shell casings,
helmets sparkle, and the leftovers of battle
bend to inevitable will of forgetfulness.
The breeze lifting your hair has lost
the stale smell stolen from the mouths
of dead men, and this *you*,
drawn together by light, silver
particles suspended in emulsion,
is freed from the thickness of the scene, frozen
in the twitch of a photographer's finger,
leaving you remembering this moment
the same way that glass remembers sand.

The Heart's Archaeology

On some fundless expedition,
you discover it beneath
a pyracantha bush
carved from the hip bone
of a long-extinct herbivore
that walked the plains on legs
a story tall. An ocarina of bone
drilled and shaped laboriously
with tools too soft to be efficient
by one primitive musician
spending night after night
squatting by the fire.
No instrument of percussion:
place this against your lips,
fill it from your lungs to sound
a note winding double helix, solo
and thready calling to the pack.

Blanche Farley

Alder Moon

for Mary Downs

Four in the afternoon and already
the moon is lying on one cheek, gazing down
on Rooster Ridge, as if she disapproves.
Machines upbraid great roots, larger than cars.
Rocks raise high the swirling dust.

This is the last cold snap that comes
to bow the daffodils, and I want to think
of Demeter receiving her wandering child.
I want to think of Lent and sacrifice
and how the alder tree will bleed when felled.

But when the walnut clock chimes four,
your face appears, stronger than legend—
that last time I saw you, your white cheek
pressed to the covers. Your pale mouth moaning.
And nothing saved, nothing risen.

Good Friday in Jasper

Feathers scattered on the hills,
   the chicken houses ripped to ruin,
      homes and industries wiped off the map—
        this is the aftermath.
At the grocery store, donation jars
   for victims are already filled.
      Everyone swaps stories
        of the random way it swept—
how one man saved his life
   by lying in a bathtub,
      while yards away a toddling child
        was flung off down the hollow.
Then the governor is riding, tight-lipped,
   in the TV chopper, over land he knows
      that knew the Cherokee,
        the settlers' axe and plow.
His face becomes a rugged ridge
   the sun won't reach. He understands
      these mountaineers.
        They will build again,
will sift the rubble, clear the slopes,
   trying not to grieve for dwellings
      lost—the family pictures
        gone for good. Hard times are not
so hard now, as they once have been,
      but old fears twist
        and burn.

Laughter

Our grandfather owned a Victrola
and a few thick records that he liked to play
summer evenings on the farmhouse porch.
Think of it—the way the children sat cross-legged
on the wide wood floor, our grandmother

dashing out the screen door,
untying her apron as the sharecroppers came.
Eight or ten of them. Black faces, white ones,
the workday's dust still in their hair.
They would stand in the yard, my mother says,
as long as the records turned,
the same songs every time.

No one complained. (Perhaps they smelled
the scuppernongs in the arbor, or Grandmother's
sweetshrubs in the yard, depending
on the season.) At last, "the laughing record" played—
played loud and lusty on the edge of darkness.

It was nothing more than a man laughing,
laughing on and on, till the notion caught
and everyone in earshot laughed hard with him.

Malaika Favorite

The End

"We are sorry to announce the end of Time"
—Time Magazine *subscription service*

You have reached the last page
Your Forever stamp
Is canceled
When you wake up
There will be no tomorrow
To anchor you to reality
Your shoes still fit
But there is nowhere to go
When the bell rings
You will not change class
But sit staring at the blackboard
Expecting an explanation
The stamps in your pocket
Floating up to the ceiling
Dangling like light bulbs
Outside everyone is watching the sky
Waiting for a thunder clap

Rupert Fike

First Memory, Grandfather's Cabin

My great-aunts shuffle through the rubble,
black pocketbooks held close, at the ready,
> They took the dining room table. Laws . . .
> They broke every window, Lord, have mercy . . .
> They tore out the walnut shelves!
I am six, confused—Who are . . . They?
The outhouse is horrifying enough
for a child mostly reared by these women,
Edwardian hold-outs, my grandmother
the one sister to marry, endure sex,
go to France with her med student husband,
who, after studying with Madam Curie,
zapped so many tumors in the New South
he was able to buy this mountain acre,
these rooms that must have once been not broken.

But "Pop" is dead now, *gone on*, they say,
his beloved place on its own slow slide,
his wife and her sisters helpless, appalled
(an increasingly favorite word),
from confronting the low-side of life.
They'd been raised in Knoxville those summer nights
James Agee preserved for all time.
Their world had been filled by manners, honor.
Reading headlines from unbought newspapers
was, I was taught, the same as stealing.
And now senseless meanness, their best family
rooms trashed, debauched by Rabun county folk,
likely the same locals Dickey would draft
to police the wild river (down two hills)
from the likes of us, Atlanta people,
a family fresh out of sober men
(my father will sell all this for bar debts).
I am the last great hope, only too late,
little more than a dress-up doll for them.
The world is changing. My aunts will soon die
the way we all do when days first go strange

then beyond redemption. Closing time.
The century's half spent, so much is too late.
Atoms have been split, radiation spilt
beyond all recall, loosed even here
into innocent June bugs and dust motes
caught in this haze over Warwoman Dell.

Commune Winter

Before we knew this would be serious
we skipped stones down the creek,
grasshopper games, death to water striders.
We sketched plans for unroofable domes
while neighbors chopped, stacked oak splits.

Days shortened yet macro and micro still spoke,
giardia burps a potent birth control,
the Mennonites' old mare (thrown in on a trade)
came up lame, her hooves so packed with thrush
the chipped-out stench brought crows thinking, *carrion!*

Canning jars didn't seal, and out on Highway 20
semis disturbed the peace with their jake brakes.
Wood smoke hung, molecules too cold to escape
scrub-oak hollows, folds in a mapped blanket
the county taxed and sometimes repossessed.

We sat za-zen, chanted *Ommmm,* and made sure
the Primitive Baptists knew about it.
Kerosene leaked on brown rice we ate anyway—
Take that, pinworms! Frozen tire ruts twisted ankles.
Fence post vultures spread wings to a brief sun.

The miller refused our Deaf Smith wheat—too hard
for his stones, he said, so we boiled wheat berries
which never once got done. Sorghum sweetened
cereal gave babies the shits. Wet oak sizzled,
put fires out; piss jars clouded the second day.

Hunger almost hurt. Distant parents, off-the-clock,
accepted charges from the curbed street world
we left for campus quads and now blighted fields,
peyote tea on solstice morning, tape-handled ax lost
beneath snow, entropy loose, uncaring.

Radical Rhetoric, 1968

We lived in college-rental shanties
just across the tracks from a hosiery mill
where actual *workers* (the word we so loved)
showed up every day in their ailing cars.
And there they were, the ones we had sworn
to *organize*, what, of course, we never tried
for they lived in far-better houses
than our listing shacks, so it would have been
the bohemian poor trying to instruct
a lower-middle-class who hated us.
Still we adhered to the notion because
it cast us in the soft light of *struggle*,
a romantic fable starring ourselves.

We were snobs, and we used drugs,
even bashing nasal inhalers with bricks
like cavemen in the driveway hungry for
that amphetamine-soaked cotton wick
(what also contained potent menthols).
O, blessed short-cut to all wisdoms!
Fully understandable for eighteen hours—
our window to cram then pass finals that,
once failed, meant a physical, Vietnam, death,
the threat that forced all-night study sessions
punctuated by deep midnight insights
never once remembered the next day,
breakthrough visions expressed through nose-holding
mentholated burps that repelled modish
art school girls who might have briefly thought us
intriguing when we hollered, "Che! Che! Che!"
to Aretha's song, when we partied
at the pace of frat boys who'd soon *exploit*
the poor *proletariat*, the damned
we so longed to save in some vague future,
the faithful who answered the mill's whistle
twice daily, its shriek sometimes making us
cheer, "Quitting Time!" in *solidarity*
when outside, if we had bothered to look,
their cars had just pulled in. It was morning,
and a new diamond dew coated the world.

Starkey Flythe, Jr.

Greeks

The fished, they wrestled,
they greased each other up,
they scraped each other down—
strigils. They fought, they
farmed, they played lyres,
flutes, they whispered
in ampitheatres which sat
twenty thousand souls
how a man killed his father
and married his mother, and how
it wasn't a particularly good idea,
the man running down the road
couldn't stop. If only we could've solved
a riddle; but what good are 'if onlies?'

They built temples, fattened
columns in the middle
to make them look the same
all the way up, down—*entasis.*
They danced on grapes, pressed
olives, sailed, slaughtered.
They made man beautiful
and woman too, though
occasionally her arms fell off.
They invented democracy—
the *whole* people, Pericles said—
imposed reason, wore bed sheets, bore
wine, water (moderation) in pleasing
shapes, *amphorae*—the Greeks had a word.
Everything was painted then, red,
yellow, blue, Aphrodite, Parthenon, kitchen
colors; statues, *stoa*, minds, all white, now.

Among the Things We Had

was a lamp, brass, maybe brass plated,
a Chinese boy who'd stopped fishing,
or had he been carrying something?
The bamboo pole with the buckets
on either end, laid down there, by his feet.
And he sat on the metal grass,
made himself comfortable, was reading,
the intensest look on his brass face,
a pigtail, coolie jacket, pajama pants.
I stared at it for hours, the kind of thing
a child wants to be, or to be in, or break,
be punished for as if being a child had rest stops
and pit falls that should be got over fast
and with a definite crash instead of being drawn out,
indefinitely.

*

The coolie leaned against the glass cylinder
where the light bulb socket was, fluted glass
so the light flowed out in rainbows,
and you could imagine the words,
how if you mispronounced a Chinese syllable
it meant midwife (whatever that was)
instead of peony (which didn't grow here).
On the top was a pagoda lid.
The glass broke first. The pagoda rested
on the naked light bulb until it got hot.
My father bought a lower watt bulb.
Then, against the wall on top the book shelf
the boy, once a lamp, became an end, leaned
and held *National Geos* and paperbacks.
I wonder where it went, not valuable
enough to steal, or beautiful enough to survive
people moving, changing tastes, broken marriages,
lares, *penates*, fire, the frayed electric cord.

We're Taking the Real Estate Exam

I'm shaking, more from cold
than fear though there's plenty
of scared running around—seven a.m.,
would be's from all over the state, futures,
commissions depending. "You want a drink?"
Martha asks me. "Good god, Martha!
It's six o'clock in the morning, I can't
even find my pencil." "Seven," she corrects.
"Here." Hands me a number two yellow, sharp.
She has that kind of mind, precise, alcohol-
razored, lips a flask disguised as an eyeglass case.
I watch her during questions that refuse to stay
on paper while she swigs, wets the tip of her pencil,
pretends myopia, far sightedness, going at it
like a safe cracker earing Fort Knox clicks.
I make sixty-five. Martha ninety-five. A veteran,
they give me five. We drink a celebratory lunch.
"Vodka's loaded with vitamin-K," she tells me.
"Reach in the back," she thumbs, driving home,
the cooler. Bottles. Cans. Mason jars, a *Cajun
martini. Cajun,* Louisiana for *more, many.*
Ice unfreezes my wrong-answer-cramped fingers.
She speeds up, never veering over the line, cold
jar to her lips, the road a foyer to all the houses
she'll sell, houses by the side of the road, houses
in gated communities where you're not allowed
to mow your grass after five o'clock Saturdays,
gothic lettered *For Sale* signs; no pink flamingos,
neighborhood parties she'll always be invited to.

Ethan Fogus

Shadow

Under the maidenhair tree
shaded in the bars of limbs.
In the rye grass we kissed,
and melted like shadows.
Once in the shaded limbs
I brushed her locked hair.
Now, I talk to the shadows
and wait by the cellar door.
No combing her brown hair,
and kissing in the rye grass.
Please, return this shadow
back to the maidenhair tree.

Gregory Fraser

End of Days

There are those who swear it will start with the sun
snapping a fiery whip, lashing the hills with flame,
while others hear men and women shrieking,

being run through by burnished swords of wind,
scalding-hot needles of rain. They say lightning
will slash open the air with its serrated blade,

and thunder gallop like blood through the gash,
spewing steam from its blazing mane,
that a blinding radiance will pour down

the sky's domed walls, painting each town
a terrible, glaring red, stripping trees
and houses bare, and somewhere it is written

that windows will be left hanging
like limpid drapes. I'm not sure if parents
still recite how some will stand at the end of days,

rapt with terror, their stunned faces running off
their faces like tears, blistered arms and legs
wrapped in bandages of pure white heat,

seared eyes in blindfolds of light. Frankly,
I don't care. To me it's nothing more
than fancy run amok. I can't believe the children

will burn like wicks on the shores of molten rivers
(formerly the streets on which they played),
that the drunkard splayed in the gutter, leaning

against the curb-wall, will have his head struck
like a match. No, the stars and planets
will never gather, raise two candescent fists,

and pummel the darkness beyond recognition,
then stretch a tight clean sheet from this horizon
to that. Still, these visions toll like bells inside

my brain, and I can't help but eavesdrop
when someone dreams aloud
of witnessing the visage of God, or some other

lucid shadow, some maker of the void It fills,
hovering the punished plain. I'll never grasp the reason
elders sigh and worry their beards

over prophetic tomes, why the wisest of women
can be found at tables lit by a single candle,
thinking its tiny torch our collective future

writ small. Yet to hear the haunting yowl
of the unspayed cat in spring, walking
her fertility's coals, or to pass a cluster of teens

puffing on cigarettes, and watch the halos
of their smoke rings warp, then vanish
into nowhere, is to gain a flickering sense

of what it suddenly might mean
to have been handed down a tale that binds
people together, twisting the many

strands of their mortal fears
into a rope that might be lowered when they fall
into the dark abysses of their making.

It's to have some notion why
the handful of survivors, scattered across
the deserted land, are predicted to go crazy,

finding it impossible to face the stark
field sprawled before their sight, and shooting
themselves toward heaven like flares.

The Stuff

The night he swerved his pick-up into a gully
and dialed me up for help, I drove out ready
to shove him into the mud-slick ditch, call him
a reckless ass, and spit in his face what I knew
he knew far better than any midnight friend—
that the stuff was going to kill him, sooner than later,
maybe someone else, maybe a family, as well—
but when at last I found him off Highway 5, chilled
and apologetic, under a moth-eaten blanket
of sky, I couldn't bring myself even to scoff
or shake my head, he seemed so small,
far off, as if seen through a telescope turned
backwards, and he was my mentor, let's not forget.

We stood for a minute in silence—he, swaying
pine-like, me looking down the road for cops,
then into the muscled distance of black hills.
I could hear the wind leaf nervously through its books,
searching on my behalf for a timely piece
of wisdom that might, miraculously, cure
the man, if only axioms hadn't died with Pope.
I don't know, he slurred, *how to thank you*,
and I came this close to saying *Quit*, but only
cracked a smile, one meant to make me appear
too worldly wise to judge. In fact, I was thinking,
judgmentally, about the beer that made him
grabby, wine that drew out song, and the bourbon

with its taste of sun-bleached leather, tightening
the belt. And earlier, I lied. I drove out planning
to bust him once, sharply, in the teeth, to watch
blood, not more regrets, trickle from his mouth.
Wasn't that the mouth that told me I could do
anything with my life, anything on the page?
Hadn't he suggested, in a poem of his own,
that our spirits are so radiant they throw shadows
of flesh and bone? *Really*, he said, *I mean it*,
but I could hardly hear him. Already,
I was on my back, keeping my hands busy
with the chains, hooking them to the frames
underneath our bumpers, working to pull him free.

Poetry Is Stupid

I was majoring in dendrology and girls,
failing both, so when my hated roommate
burst in from English class, slammed
down his book bag and declared, *Poetry
is stupid—it does nothing for the world*,

I knew I'd found my calling. One
look at his composition, scrawled in red
like a field at Maldon, I smirked and hit
the stacks, came back loaded down:
Milton, Dickinson, Auden, Rich.

He whined for days, calling the teacher
idiot, bitch, recounting his unbroken string
of high-school As. *Ou sont les neiges d'antan?*
I despised his loafers, Izod shirts, smooth
persuasion of hair, and envied with a numbing ache

the queue of beauties he ushered in, cueing me,
with a nod, to beat it. I'd slump off
to the Student Center, pore through *Howl*,
Homeric Hymns, repeating the mantra
beneath my breath, *Poetry is stupid . . .*

Second term, I traded *pinus nigra*
for Robert Frost, *catalpa speciosa*
for Sexton and Plath. And slowly, as middle
Pennsylvania thawed, the notebooks filled:
Tonight, I lose my birth weight in sweat

alone, sip the matter of my fall in rye,
chew the cattle's flesh, spin like a spider
the lace of verse . . . Recitation
vexed the jerk—*Cut that shit*, he'd snap,
from his annexed two-thirds of our space.

Rumor has it he made a killing
in the dot-com boom. They say
he even clanged the bell one morning
at the stock exchange—gross tintinnabulations.
In my mind's eye, though, I place him

in a smaller scene, purchasing a birthday
gift for his wife (the third). He browses
down the wrong aisle in a Barnes & Noble,
and spotting my name along one spine,
double-takes and says out loud: *Hey,*

I roomed with that hand-job freshman year.
Then he cracks the slender volume, peruses
till he finds the poem—this poem—dedicated
to none other than him: my adversary,
my antonym, my Unferth, my muse.

Kerri French

Dear Hands,

I cannot wake up. Some nights, a green porch
is all that's left, rain dripping through blue lights.
Everywhere, a new name. Dear Hotel, I cannot

unhinge the hour. The streets are without bridges,
the ceiling without stars. We moved against.
We touched beside. Some nights, he's gone, still

circling the river where once we kissed, crawled,
were through with the other. Dear January, some say
we swallowed winter, held our bodies in snow.

Dear Envelope, it was the neck's only migration.
Some nights, insects crash through the window
and we're closer to sky again, colorless currents.

Dear Cities, I cannot trace the edges. Dear
Leaves, I cannot recall the red. Dear Broken,
Dear Near, Dear Always, Dear Nothing—I cannot.

Tobacco

We cannot get rid of the smell:
kitchen rising with bread

baked half an hour too long,
the weeds of field like crust

growing into the recess of oven.
All around us the sun shakes

leaves so bright they burn a green
flame over the skirts of land.

Out back, rows of crops
sweep themselves into tidy

borders of sky. When no one
is looking, they speak

through stalk rumblings of sound,
curling their stem of tongues

like fists through air.
Sleepwalking, they travel

at night through the strains
of drought, digging beneath dirt

and roots in search of some way
to keep breathing out—

the inhale, exhale
of the obtruding seasons.

Alice Friman

Troubled Interiors

When fish wake in the sea
fin-shaken by whim
or tide, what a confusion—
subject as they are to the wee
switch in the brain that makes
permanently opened eyes see
or not. But how enviable the dreams.
Lidless projections on big wet screens,
unlike our own troubled interiors.

My mother too, in the high hours
of her dying, could not close her eyes.
The once-bright hazel, transfixed
under a yellowish glaze. The lower lids
drooping inside out like buntings
of raw meat. Animal under the ice,
frozen in sight of the hole. I could not look.

Fish stare, stare of the all-knowing,
stare of retribution—or was that imagined—
as I laid a cool wet cloth over her eyes.
For her comfort, I said. Then holding her hand
and singing the songs she always sung to me,
I sang her, blindfolded, out of this world.

A good daughter? Let me tell you.
The eye of ice flings enough light to read by.
Even now, six years later, lying here in the dark,
I can still make out the words. *Liar. Fraud.*

Visiting Flannery

Andalusia

Across the pond and up the hill
from where I sit, the lady's house—
her room of crutches and ugly drapes,
the flat and sorry pillow. Her Royal
turned for concentration to a wall.

I come often, greet the orphaned space,
wave when I leave. But today, Good Friday,
I wonder what she'd think—this Yankee
heretic, two generations from steerage,
scribbling by her pond across from
the screened-in porch where afternoons
she'd rest, enjoying her peahens'
strut and feed. How old is too young
with so much left to do? Even the barn,
reliving her story of what happened there,
is buckled to its knees.

Suddenly, a flash from the water—
fish or frog—and I too late
to catch the shine. The Georgia sun
dizzies my head and I am no saint.
Nor was she, although there's some
who'd unsalt the stew to make her one.
Still, I like to imagine—before the final
transfusions and the ACTH that
ballooned her face past recognition—
the two of us sitting here, watching the trees
sway upside down in sky-water, ecstatic
in the bright kingdom she refracted in a drop.

Funny how two pair of eyes fifty years apart
make one in sight: a country pond
floats a heaven, and patches of trillium
spread their whites, laying a cloth for Easter.
She smirks. Easy imagery. We do not speak,
both knowing what won't sustain when clouds
roar in like trouble, the trillium inching
toward water, fluttering like the unbaptized
lost, or the ghost pages of an unwritten book.

The Night I Saw Saturn

Crossing the Pacific, flying backward
into perpetual night, and all night
one light on in the plane, a young man
beneath, scribbling. I am looking out
the window, the glass prism that shatters
the stars, and we at thirty thousand feet
not flying up but seemingly across
and headed straight toward it—Orpheus
of the night sky—the rock that sings.

What is he writing, that man
who can't sleep so doesn't even try,
stuck in an inner section, unable
to indulge in a window reverie, leaning
his head as I do against the glass?

The night I saw Saturn was because
I pleaded. *Before I die I want to see. . .*
and the astronomer complied, there
on the top of Mauna Kea, and me
shivering in all the clothes I had
and hanging on because I couldn't
see my feet, so dark it was as I set
my eye to the metal eyepiece.
Then, true to the pictures in my
schoolbooks or the planetarium's
mockup, only luminous, radiating
more energy into space than received
from the sun. Ah Saturn, grandpa
of Love, what do scientists know
of the light that lights the pearl?
Sovereign of contradiction, beauty's
absolute, cold white and burning in the sky.

And now, this man, the only light
in the plane, ringed by huddles of sleepers
as if he were guardian of the oblivious
awake for us all. How furiously
he bends to his work. How lovely
the light lingering on the shock of his hair
holds him—incandescent—reflecting in rings.

Erin Ganaway

Passing

You clutch a handkerchief like
a fulvous leaf clinging to a limb,

and I imagine that fragile linen
must feel the pulse of all your life,

the way you tap-danced on a chair
while waiting for a pound cake to rise,

the way you sung us up a stepladder
to a farm-sink bath on those sunshine

mountain evenings, the way you
taught us to snap beans in the moonlight.

We drifted to your hushed crooning,
the low rumble of our rocking,

but now I rock by your bedside,
place a palm to your cheek,

feel the warmth of your new life
radiating from your body.

Swaddled in a homemade quilt,
you glow like you have crossed over,

your face slack-peaceful as a child.
Maybe you see what is out there,

maybe you are skimming the
tips of stars with your hemline,

maybe you are dancing the
Charleston on the wisp of a cloud.

Sea Cleft

It smells of darkness in the cleft
of boulder where you used to lay

stretched out like a washed up eel,
eyes slanting into a sun glittering

off water like fizzling sparklers,
your knuckles chafed raw, bright white

as sea foam, you fingered a cigarette, cocked
your ear at a mournful fog horn, watched

the waves topple in like a hill of broken
gravestones, leaving their parenthetical

marks in the sand. And the way you
smiled at me, I thought for certain you

felt at home, that you would not leave me to
shoulder the cold breath of this scissure alone.

Crustose

Suppose your heart has grown small and bitter
as a wild strawberry, what once was succulent,

now tasteless, even the thrumming of the ocean
fails to move you. Once, the surf spiked the child-

hairs of your calves. Once, your thighs scuffed
fragmented scallop shells and errant claws of crabs.

What desperation is this dry mouth of words, this
numbing headlessness. Now there are stale mint

cigarettes that taste of old dental floss, beer left
to warm in a tepid spring. Now there are wilted

dandelions and silvered lavender buds too weak
to blossom. What once kept you turning now

leaves you bent, like holding hands with a cactus,
like waiting for something to perforate the veil.

Mac Gay

Pluto's Despair

It must have felt somewhat
like having another manuscript
rejected; or being taken out
of the starting lineup; or
the trauma of learning
the dark spot on your lung
is of dour and grave concern.
Heck, here you've been
a-list for years, part and
parcel of the pantheon,
"one of the nine best ever,"
according to the old *Almanac
of Science*, and though
nowhere near the largest,
certainly the most distant,
the most cryptic and aloof,
secluded in the hinterlands,
enigmatic as Salinger.

So was it chance that did
you in, or bad astrology,
or simply just your own
faux-pas: something you did
or did not do? Maybe
better attendance at those
tedious planetary meetings;
maybe some condescending
coolness towards the others.
But it wasn't your colleagues
that booted you out, no—
it was the scientists, those
specks with their galactic minds:
meddlers that measure us all.

Roberta George

Three o

Three o'clock in the morning,
the hour of despair,
I take out my rosary,
the red one blessed by Pope Paul.
It came in a case with his picture
and has his image graven on
the juncture where that
whole business of Paters
and Aves begins.

My niece, Mary Jo, gave it
to me after her wedding—
that whole story I can't tell
because it's not mine.

But, anyway, I press
the Pope's face in the
metal into my forehead
and ask God to give me
the mind of Pope Paul.
After all, don't you think
he grew weary of all that
ritual, of traipsing around
in robes with that thing
on his head. Just as you've
grown so tired of whatever you do
every day in the same way,
every day in the same way.

Then I recite the prayers,
not thinking the words,
just fingering the red beads, and
over and over wrapping
white circles around
the ones I love and the ones
I hate and even their pets because
I see them all, all in their houses,
all in their beds, all asleep.

I start high up in the nation,
in New York State, then come down
through Georgia, and then
through Florida to the Keys, where
nobody I know lives anymore.
And then to the West Coast
where my sisters are doing
what they did 30 years ago
selling pot, but this time—maybe—
it's almost legal.

And I wonder what good does it do,
the Memorare said nine times
at the end of the rosary
for all the ones I know with cancer
and all the ones I don't know
but hear about from my son, the nurse.

And I wonder about a mysterious
God, who would love sorrow
so much, and pain and me,
and the rain in the night
bowing down the trees,
and the rosary counted out by a
doubter, like the dogs barking
across the way, while the dog
in the house is silent.

Sarah Gordon

Narrative

The tree the storm
uprooted, a tall spruce,
leans on sister pines,
its mound of root and earth
catching the sunlight
each morning,
as I make my way
down the road and back.
Coming and going,
I see the large tree,
its underpinnings
exposed to a light
that finds nothing else
in these woods.
I want to make meaning
of this scene,
I want to say there's
a parable here, though
when I reconnoiter
I can't quite slide into
the arc of narrative,
or, more precisely,
see how it all begins
in the first place,
so as to get caught up
in the telling of it,
the story of the soul
that's singled out,
say Saul on the road,
that third figure hustling
along on the way
to Emmaus, Hazel Motes
standing on his ratcolored
car under the streetlight
preaching to himself,
or Obadiah Elihue
ransacking the book
of tattoos, coming home
sore and proud.
Sure, what's in the light
always catches our eye,
but a story, by God,
a story that fans out
the heart and quickens
the dead, now that
is something else
entirely.

Acts of Love

She approached the painting
reverently, as had many another,
and when she stood before its large white
center inside the large white edge,
she kissed it, a chaste closed-mouth
kewpie-doll smack of Sunlit Bronze
changing it forever,
or so the restorers concluded
when they could not remove
the lipsticked shape.
An act of love, she said.

How not to understand
that impulse, the simple desire
to claim and connect,
imprint or, for that matter,
be imprinted, to welcome
the stinging, needling tattoo?
Don't skies beg to be clouded,
water to be stirred?
My sweet friend Laurie, dead now
these five years, declared at thirty
she wanted crowsfeet
to inscribe her aging skin,
an outward and visible sign
of her grand embrace of life.

Why does the cat leap
onto the middle
of taut, fresh sheets?
What makes the generals
stride onto the desert,
scoring the pristine sand?
Why is passion colored purple?
And flaunted?
Does the forehead ask
to be blessed, the back
to be lashed?
Nature abhors a vacuum
or adores it.
In the margins
of all my childhood books,
I scrawled my name.

A Call to Prophecy

When he first knew something was wrong
he saw double out of his right eye,
and, tempted again and again to confirm it,
he kept moving his head in that direction,
a torturous pleasure, like tongue to gum
beneath the aching tooth.
Oh, he knew that something
was horribly amiss, everything twinned
as though shot through with some potent
fertility drug, landscape piled on landscape,
friends cloned on the periphery,
their narcissists' dreams come true.

Then he began to feel a slight pressure
near his left temporal lobe
as though a finger were insinuating itself
deep into his head and staying there.
Perhaps he'd been reading too much,
the brain irritably shaking off
all those words as one shakes out
a wet rag or a rainy umbrella at the door
or as one would like to slam
that door on all the uninvited guests
moving through his rooms, coughing,
laughing, telling their stale stories,
just asking for it, his sharp rebuke.

When first he stumbled, he thought little of it,
though his palms were raw from catching
his body on the pavement, raising himself
upright again, believing he'd tripped
on a shoelace, some threatening idea.
He looked to see if anybody saw.
No, but he was stiff for days afterward.
Unfolding himself on the soft couch,
he knew he needed to rise and walk
to prove that he could put one foot
in front of the other (that was all it was),
at least as far as the bend in the road.
Instead, he dreamed of the land,

a dry and compromised field
stretching into the horizon and planted
with plowshares and rusty engines,
tongued with green sprouts, thin
reminders of life next the cleavage
of earth, her wrinkled breasts,
her flaccid arms that will not hold
this metaphor, that will not hold
his dream, as he wakes into danger,
the sound of water running
water running somewhere.

G.R. Greenbaum

At the Gates of Dachau

We approached its gates
just outside Munich, city of culture.
But it was a Monday, and this "museum"
was closed.

The guards allowed us to enter
where no Jew of the dark
past had entered by choice,
this final innocence.

With sad legs, we crossed the outlines
of razed barracks, where tier upon tier
of wasted bodies had once lain within,
across barren fields to the crematoria.

At the ovens, we left our daughter's poem
of the yellow star that follows us
and in turmoil viewed cruel photos,
their efficient systems.

We crossed back, and as the gates closed behind us,
I reached for my purse, but it was not on my arm—
rather left beside my sorrow near the ovens,
ones I could have once departed as ashes.

Again we knocked at the gates.
Another guard, a huge, menacing man
who might well have transported me
to the showers, zyklon, rising smoke,

took us to that place where we had paid homage
to the incinerated—where my identity
had lingered in its emotional cacophony,
my purse there with its document of passage.

Sîan Griffiths

Fistful

The dead can be very useful sometimes.
    —Clint Eastwood, A Fistful of Dollars

Sometimes, it's all about how you wear your poncho,
or the layering of dust on your boots.

or how you sit a bucking mule
while five men scoff from a high-barred gate.

Where words unhinge from speaking mouths,
it's useful to be the man with no name
or the dark-eyed woman, clamped in a locket that laments its own opening.

Engineer the corpses,
and the dead are only sleeping,
secrets ever-burning on their cold parched lips.

All the Winchesters, all the Remingtons,
all the six-guns unholstered in this border town
are not enough to kill the dead;
their stories hide in the sheepskin vests
of the nameless living.

Proud Flesh

proud flesh. [See proud a. 7d (b).] Overgrown flesh arising from excessive granulation
upon, or around the edges of, a healing wound.
—Oxford English Dictionary, 2nd edition

Outside, the sun illuminates pasture grass,
Blade veins dark, stretching tall to rough clipped edges
Where horse teeth have been the only scythe.
Inside, in darkness: the stall walls painted black
Offer no reflection of the outside light.

By the single incandescent bulb caged
In wire above the barn's rough door, I, razor
In hand, shave back the new-grown, exuberant flesh
Off the leg that never did hold still. It quivers,
Blood running in thick tracks from hock to hoof.
The shadows of wire stripe us in darkness.
Against every equine instinct, he does not kick.

This is what love is:
Spattered with blood and bits of flesh
New-grown and pale as grubs. I cut and cut.
My thighs quiver, too, my back burns, my eyes
Blur, this is taking too long and I cut.

Scars are thick-skinned, brutal, binding. I
Cannot let it end this way. A month since
He wrapped himself in hotwire—him, the horse
Who never tested a fence in his life.
Now, long past showing, long past riding,
I preserve what "best" there is left.

He's done the same for me.
Divorce is its own kind of wire, binding.
There were days, too many, when I got up only to ride, days
When I went to bed right after, straw
And dirt still crusting my breeches.

He nickered to see me, through all that darkness,
Jumped every fence I pointed him at.
The sharp joy that filled his big heart
Cut me quick and steady until it bared
Enervated flesh again, opening me to feel.

Persistence of Geese

You find a goose lying on your belly,
another kind of nest.
Her webbed feet press
your vulnerable skin;
the loft of her down
brushes with your breath.
The body of her lighter than the thought of her.

It isn't until her neck arcs towards you
and she takes your nose in her bill
that you realize this has all happened before.

You try the usual tricks:
stroke the wings and offer the stale oyster crackers
you keep close at hand for these occasions.
Still: her small teeth embedded in your cartilage,
her moist tongue resting against your nostril,
her peering, impenetrable black eye,
which looks more like a bead on your mother's last dress
than you are quite comfortable with.

You pull on your jeans, your sneakers,
button her under your overcoat,
and visit the butcher who has helped you out
of these messes before.

He is able to remove all but the head,
sending you home with paper-wrapped cutlets
for the deep-freeze. The packages
are surprisingly heavy, as is the body-less head.

You will grow used
to these weights, like so many others:
the snout dangling from your left ear lobe,
the muzzle, an epaulet on your shoulder,
the lips around each toe.

Anthony Grooms

In Rousseau's Garden

A red sun hangs
Over the black, verdant jungle
Beneath the towering cycads
Among the lotus blossoms, the sansevierias and agave,
Between the columns of flowering cereus,
An ocelot attacks my silhouette

I never expected
That my death would come even before I was born
Dreamt of by a Frenchman
And sold for money

I have memories of its coming,
Of time flowing backwards like an eddy
Rousseau caught it in his strokes:
Feline—*Feline of the yellow fang*
And me running like twilight
From the thing the artist knows

The Slave Houses at Green Springs, Virginia

The hills, the round-capped hills of sea-green hay
And the gabled farm houses with curving cedar-lined drives—
They are here. St. John's Chapel with stained glass, ginger
lace eaves and trumpet vine wound
Around its fence seems ephemeral. But it is still here.

The Green Springs Spa has dried up, but the deep
Wood of oak, ivy, jewelweed in the marshes,
The one lane bridge on the gravel road through
Groves of Osage orange, and bordering the fields,
The Queen Anne's lace, they are all still here as it was.

Ionia, Sylvania, and Prospect Hill, the handsome
Manor houses are marked by Eighteenth Century
Charm. With chimneys Georgian balanced, they stand
On their lawns like monuments. In the sky,
Fair-weather cumulus.

And the slave houses are here, too, in all
This charm that could not have been
Without slaves. At Noland's you see them,
One-windowed shanties, painted now, the slaves
Gone. But not gone far.

Linda Lee Harper

Final Cut

One small scratch widens,
ulcerates into something
almost beautiful red and white,
a gorge, a chasm, a window
into the body surrendering,
even tape not holding it together.
Stitches? No option that this heart,
frail as papyrus,
can tolerate and survive,
the cut's two bruised lips
futilely migrating
toward each other,
contracting, advancing,
death's little pucker,
kiss, kiss.

Karen Head

Part of the Bargain

"Take a shiny quarter for it?"
she clutched my left ring finger
caressing the wart I wanted rid of.
She had an eye twitch
as if a rapid wink had possessed her.
I couldn't imagine why
this old crone would want my wart
how exactly she would get it,
but I was thirteen and desperate,
tired of the cute boys, ugly ones too,
saying I was out kissing frogs,
calling me a witch.
So, when Granny offered
to sneak me over to the conjure woman
while my mama was running errands
I was game, eager even,
just didn't realize I'd be selling
a part of myself.

Standing there on that back porch
overhanging a creek,
I could hear the croaking
as I took the quarter
and one last look at my wart.
"Belongs to me now, quit your looking."
Her eye no longer twitched.
She turned back into her shack,
and Papa drove us home.

Next day, the wart was gone
and for the first time in my life
I felt I'd sold out,
gave away my magic for nearly nothing.

M. Ayodele Heath

On Closing Woodruff Park, Atlanta

(for renovation for the 1996 Summer Olympics)

exhaling . . .
                    icicle-clad, sky-blue breath
            inhaling . . .
                                    sharp, cold metallic abandon . . .

They've closed Woodruff Park where, last summer,
    Brother Johnson, in a striped bow-tie
            one of the brothers from The Nation gave him
            at the shelter back in '87 (he was so proud),
            preached his daily sermon to a crowd
            of no fewer than two hundred
            about *the power of Black Nationalism*
            & how *Geronimo Pratt is still in prison*
            & *Mumia Abu Jamal still ain't free*; and

    Sister Mabel *Boydidyoucombyohairthismawnin?* Davis
        was always makin sho the city clean
        when all dem White folks n' Japs come in 1996.
        You don't want dem goin back n' tellin' dey people
        Atlanta's a nasty city wit trash all ovah da ground.
        I mean you wouldn't invite company 'round
        yo house if you hadn't cleaned up, wouldya? unaware
        of her pending eviction notice
        as she picked up a policeman's
        abandoned Dunkin' Donuts bag; and

    Mister Haynes (he nothing to lose, I a friend to gain)
        bet me lunch he could checkmate me
        in ten moves (it only took seven)
        & I bought him a sandwich at Michael's Deli.
        Best meal I had since Hosea's dinnah last Christmas season.
        Turkey & Swiss. No pork. Brother Johnson say
        dat's blue-eyed devil food. With ridged corn chips.
        Man, I ain't had dese in . . .

a luxury I guess
        when you are homeless—
                when your home
        address is
Woodruff Park.

All that hair must be hot
        I thought. But
                it must be warm
        in the winter (in this air
that hurts to breathe.)

I wonder
        if Black turns to blue
                when you're that cold,
        old, low & forgotten
by this progressive city of lofty,
        glass skyscrapers
                full of stonethrowers
        who've never walked a mile
even in their own shoes.

Holding the mayor's free
        one-way bus ticket
                to AnywhereButHere
        if you'll just sign this contract
that you'll never come back.

Heartless January
    shrilling
            like an angry woman
    You are nothing
in your ear.

I wonder
where they live
now

Eye of the Beholder

—after seeing the Without Sanctuary exhibit

Beauty in things exists in the mind which contemplates them.
—David Hume, from "Essays," Of Tragedy

a wave of ten
thousand foaming white

men stormed
a georgia

jail & lynched
a colored boy

in june rain
for a smile (which

he did commit) as he
     hung

from a yellow traffic
light—noose

bearing all
their weight—not one

said Stop, but
     one

took
a picture

Sara Henning

Eros

I look for rain lacquering
        the hymnal of dirt—
                rain, against the sky, bone shards.

                Grass erodes, lilies drift,
                        bodies found face down
                                in lakewater.

Which world do
        they belong to that makes them
                deathless,

                a journey back to the world
                        unlivable,
                                beginning of the story

where the bulbs
        warmed between your fingers
                as you labored.

                When each uproots the soil
                        like a planet shapeshifting,
                                is when I know its beauty—

refractive child of the soil,
        deep-kissed
                by tundra.

Lisa Hodgens

When You Come

–after Kimiko Hahn

This gladness can be a color: fire,
let's call it, or oxblood, say, or wine.

Your first painting after the sorrow
brushed crimson a blackbird wing in flight

against the russet October light
of the city where we met. Your next

gift—a bouquet of scarlet dahlias,
snipped from your garden, placed in a vase.

The wraiths that marked your drawings have fled,
maroons that haunted your canvases

gone. The raven you saw when you closed
your eyes has flown to feast on others'

despair. Your house is now a refuge,
your garden a place of peace. In your

dream, fox cubs tumble harmlessly
beneath apple-heavy boughs. You sleep

quietly as never before, then
spill melons, plums, rosefire at my door.

Uweyu Nvya

High Falls, 1817

Uweyu Nvya is Cherokee (phonetic)
for "river stone"; High Falls is located
in what is now northern Alabama.

Setting down her basket of hickory nuts,
chestnuts, persimmons, and muscadines,
gathered under an early autumn sun,
a young Tsalagi woman steals time.

She rests her weariness at the river
rock, leans over the clear water, gazing
at silver minnows schooling in shallows.
Stone warming her body, she witnesses

the world's wild purpose: white walnuts sprinkling
a green field; two squirrels jostling pine cones
into the river; jagged-edged shards of ancient
mountains smoothing into river stones.

When a cooling breeze brushes the down on
her neck, she cups her hands in the water
to drink. Then touching her lips to warm gray rock,
she gives thanks for her moment of peace.

Leaves rustle in the forest canopy,
shadows move easily across the ground,
a wolf slips away from the sacred sight:
a woman embraced by a stone.

Karen Paul Holmes

Singing with Beethoven

Leaving Brasstown
my car moves past twilight,
dusk enough
to sense fields with dark cattle shapes,
a black-mountain backdrop.
I turn on the radio, crack windows—
Music, nature mingle in cool air,
cricket song merges with "Ode to Joy."

Now, night enough
that my headlights end in nothingness,
I have to trust
where the curving road goes.
For a moment
I fixate on the void,

a blue shiver travels my spine.

Then Beethoven heartens me.
Seek beyond the starry canopy!
I hit the pedal and drive on home,
belting it out like a fat soprano.

Randall Horton

Wail the Sinner

after charles johnson's portrait going to church

not even two hours
    out the juke-joint
bourbon breathed
        lil jimmy
up from the choir box rose
sangin' *"precious*
        lawd"
still he reeked the first note
sister ola rae cried   her fan
      swung
religiously the wail
& ensuing moan
    mirrored the preacher's
scream reproduced a bluemythography
        of sweat
but creation's arms
          extended
further back up through
lil jimmy's rendition
      of *going*
to church he migrated
momentarily   south-
      westward
pines faced the blue wood house
yards from an oxcart
    rolling
down clay dirt road
      to the congregation
simply   naïve
jimmy's solo a call
    few could hear
even when he shouted.

James Hudson

The Feel of Fall

It was the aimless buzzing of a fly
that had him raise a dull, despondent, eye—
watch the captive bounce against the pane
until it whirled to freedom when he raised the frame,

and from the window saw the church's spire
against a hill that maples set afire,
stubbled field that reached a tumbled mill
where carefree boys shied stones across the rill;

saw smoke trails, sungilt, blown from farmer's fire
that burned dead thistle, vetch and briar
before the barn, where piles of pumpkins stood,
an orange facing to its weathered wood.

He found in all a concord, earth and man—
there the healing of his mood began.

T.R. Hummer

Slow Train through Georgia

The mist that rises from this river solidifies the air
Underneath the rusty trestle where a train has come and gone.
It is the precipitate of the chemical morning, dumped
Unceremoniously into the clear solution of a summer night.
Hours earlier, the midnight freight detonated under starlight
Three hours late and thundering toward Birmingham, the red glow
Of the steel mills, the tincture of that constant dawn.
But now the air shuts down. Now the distant whistles of the morning shift
Into the throats of mockingbirds, and the sun works
Its electrolytic clarity from the top down, starting with the ozone.
The mist rising off the muddy little river curves south beyond the bridge.
It follows the water, of which you might be tempted to imagine
It is the astral body, downstream toward the Gulf—
Because you want to believe in the soul of the river, don't you,
You want a name and a positive destination
For this ghostly swath like a scar between banks of new-leafed oaks,
As if the world had a center and you were standing in it,
As if everything turning were your own self-evident revolution.
But watch this scene long enough and the sun
Will defeat you, the beautiful obscurity of the mist
Will dilute and disappear. Already the revelation is working
Its inevitable way toward you from the upper atmosphere. Soon
The oil-scummed image of the surface of the river will superimpose
Its visionary dreariness on what you can see of the earth:
Red clay, a distant cotton field, the tin roof of a tenant house
Where morning touches a mirror and moves at the constant speed of light
To touch the face of the sleeping man who stirs and touches his wife
Who is awake already, worrying over breakfast, remembering
The deep-night noise of the train that stopped
Whatever dream she might have had, the double blackness
Of coal-heaped gondolas hours after midnight, the anonymous steel
Of wheels against greased rails, inhuman, turning—like everything she knows
About God and politics—against her, going nowhere.

Friendly Fire

*Land war will require the most complex
combat flying ever flown, with more
tragedies of friendly fire inevitable.*
                    —CNN newscast, 2/4/91

Heraclitean, for instance: the world as a gaseous
Shimmer, like afterburner fumes in the oily night sky
Outside Carbondale, where lovers pass through the flux
Of the heart's napalm—or alchemical: the transformative image
Of the sun over Dallas, antiseptic if you could touch it,
Tritely ætherial, the volatile gold of gas-well burn-off
On the freeway's horizon, cauterizing, uncorrupting bone—
We could imagine anything. Suppose we pulled a lever
And every carburetor in Charlottesville
Detonated in a transcendental rush of mustard gas
And oxyacetylene? What would we think we were seeing?
What residue would remain?
                                        I think it would be elemental.
I think it would be pure. I think it would give off the smell
Of brass, chrysanthemum, caustic old velour—
Or that strange metallic odor that drags my grandmother's face
Up from the flare of my neurons, where the innocent dead all go:
A bombed-out country no body belongs to, untouchable, chemical, clean.

Apocatastasis Foretold in the Shape of a Canvas of Smoke

At the left edge of the field of vision, a stooped woman dumps
Steaming water from her galvanized bucket against a granite wall.
In this meditation, she might be an emblem of genocide

Or simply somebody's grandmother dumping dishwater in the snow.
Gray earth, gray sky—the brushstroke of the horizon visible
Only to someone who knows what to look for, pure

Transparent style. The water is a soapy broth of tea dregs,
Grease, and lye, which the wormy dog that hides
Under her skirt licks from the frozen stones. Its every gesture

Is an archetype, something that could be perfectly described only
In Indo-European. In the middle distance, from the indistinct
Shadow of a minor mountain, there is hazy motion, possibly an army:

The sound of leather groaning, silk-muffled hammers
Of the temple builders, adze-chafe, pneumatic saws, the crack
Of a splintering axletree. The dog's ruff is the same shade of silver

As the metal of her bucket, and the water the bucket holds,
And the vapor that rises off the frost-etched stone of the wall.
Her old dress bunches at her belly in an intaglio like stretch marks.

She had children, and those children died. She had children,
And those children had children. Where is the nostalgia
For humanity? Where are all the stories we have learned

To interpret so perfectly? You may think there is tragedy here,
But this is only the beginning. In the gunpowder haze that lifts
Over the boundary-ridge, and in the bucket's mural of steam,

The characters gather: a man who lifts his handful of blood
To the vacuous spirit he knows is his mother, and she drinks
And speaks his name, and is oblivion. Look

Where the machinery of heaven drags form after form
Out of this sarcophagus God carved from the onyx cliff-face of being
And hinged with elaborate craftsmanship into the joinery of her spine,

So when the latch clicks and the lid of her body swings open,
Another rises luminous and whole into the expanse of unconcealment.
It comes to almost nothing. Winter is here, and the half-starved

Cattle still give milk, though it is thin, with a tinge of vein-blue.
February sleet spits on flagstones with the noise a bronze knife makes
Against hickory. The carver at his bench is gouging another bowl

For goats' blood, while the dog in the culvert gnaws
Whatever rat he can find, then curls his carcass in on itself
Like a Möbius strip for warmth, everything drawn together.

Mike James

I Used to Dream of Becoming the Village Idiot

The children would toss apples at me
And I would eat the apples

Sometimes I would take the apples
To a kind matron
(A blacksmith's wife)
She would bake me an apple pie

No one would throw the apple pie at me
I would eat all of it
Alone
Beneath a tree
In a field far away from the children

At night the stars would stay in place
Not even the wind would make them blink

Christopher Jelley

Barrier Island

I walk an ebb-tide beach
past hidden turtle troves, above
the cove where cautious lovers used to meet.
Wind, salt, spray. Seabirds play—
Flesh and feather hung forever.

I pluck a bone of sun-bleached
oak from a dune-killed grove,
etch a string of tear drop pearls
into wet sand, just beyond
the footprints circling home.

One year ago along this reach
I set your ghost to rove.
Scattered the earth, cast gray ash
upon the water's green. Words
scribbled out to sea.

Gordon Johnston *For Maura — my sister.*
Thanks for coming.
Gordon Johnston
11/9/13

Bear

From the deep shade under the laurel an air
　a breath the blurred beam of animal vision
　　lands on him, a man of forty in worn-out woods

He turns his head and each sees and scents
　the other in a second that has no center,
　　that is focused and eternal and over

The oldest paths in their bodies open and he
　is anciently human in his loafers and sweat
　　which strangle her their smell like the taste

of brass crowding all she knows out of her dim
　bear brain so that she rises huffing from rooting
　　the grubs out of the rotted log and because he

stops because he freezes as he sees her the way a threat
　to a cub would freeze she drops again goes into motion
　　What he thinks is not that ten years have passed since he

has walked in the woods not that she smells like his ex-wife's
　schnauzer not even that he will die now what he thinks is PBS
　　a televised ranger saying Bluff charge and You shouldn't run and

he doesn't but he has flinched and she is upslope of him a little
　she is already there and by the time the TV of memory says Fall and he
　　does she is striking him snout-first knocking him backwards his palms

grazing her jowl fur in a touch that in slo-mo would be tender
　and he smells the loam along her muzzle loam of hunger so that
　　that smell is what he curls around fetal on the gravel path born

again His glands open his body perceiving that there is nothing to save
　as her teeth touch together through the tail of his shirt her breath
　　on his lower back the nose dry and moving exactly like a dog's blowing

at his neck his forehead where it meets his knees his shoes which
　he doesn't know are saving him because yesterday he had them polished
　　and the tang in them is like a blunt blow between her eyes He feels

her weight gone from the ground around him his eyes open in the circle
　he has made of himself and already he loves her who has let him live.

137

Crutches

In high school I loved every girl who had them, fell for little fingers
curled around the foam rubber grips, for the chunky plaster cast

full as a dance card with names. Bent-knee peep show
of toes glossed Candy Apple, nails a row of shrinking red faces

like those secretly hollow dolls that nest inside each other.
Karen Wynn fringed the cut leg of her Levis over her cast,

teasing the threads fine as mohair till they tickled my dreams.
She swung between them from Chorus to Chemistry,

ticking *crutch-tip, toe, crutch-tip, toe* till I went sick with wishing,
my heart knocking to her slow rhythm. *Why* worried me: it was

the odd leverage, I guess—the way they walked on palms and armpits,
it pried at my ribs. Their casts were public as our paint rock,

where at night little groups of us sprayed names, love,
and bonehead wit in big, first-grade letters. A hurt girl's

homeroom would kneel one at a time and scribble:
inside, her fibula, in the warm grip of girl muscle, knit.

All I knew to write was my crooked name, nowhere near her toes,
But in the middle, where the snow of plaster was deepest,

where, itching under my gray lead name, she might lay her hand.

Hooters Girls

Hooters girls do not understand us better,
      but they share out something kept back from unloved men.
They bear steaming platters and out of their own need
      suffer our smallness, dressing for us as clowns do for children,
        out of worn-out sympathy.
We want only our mothers young again, our womb-life, that one ime
      when we were held as close as we wanted to be.
The moment of conception, maybe, is what we wish for, beyond,
      before,
when the world was a mother, milk and breath moving through us
      in tides. We had no arms to hold our mothers with.
        Only her inner world mattered.
We lived there, sunlight through blood, without knowing
      what we knew. We were women.
Now we have forgotten everything.

Some want us to learn again. Not Hooters girls.
      They have given up, though they still bring us tiny wings,
        folded and golden.
We try and simplify need into lust, to articulate loss .
      by praising tits and ass. Deaf to our own prayers.

Seaborn Jones

Semper Fi

For Frank Kern

Drunk again. Ear to the talking bone.
Spinning numbers, area codes, crossing time zones
Chicago, Memphis, San Francisco.
The combinations that unlock voices out of the past
after midnight, saying, "Yes, yes, I think I remember,
I was asleep, call back."

Of the four Bob Olivos I spoke with in New York
none of whom were the Bob Olivo I know
the fallen Warhol Super-Star
selling hot dogs at Yankee Stadium.

I call Larry in North Carolina but reach a Mr. William O. Foster
in Phoenix Arizona, who hangs up.

I call Larry again. Larry hangs up.
I try Yankee Stadium.

I call my ex-wife in Los Angeles. I call my daughter in Atlanta.
I call people who owe me money. I call people that I owe money.

I call my father, mother, brother, sister, aunts, uncles,
nieces, nephews, cousins. I get a recorded message from
a church in Detroit. I call four Bob Olivos again
to make sure.

For God's sake, is anybody in America awake?
I've done my best but they've all fallen in the dreaming.
The talking bone says, "Parris Island, South Carolina, Sgt. Baker
speaking." I ask if the Marines are awake. "Yes Sir" he says,
"Twenty-four hours a day."

I tell him about Yankee Stadium, my wife, my daughter. . .

"You're drunk," he says. "I'm hanging up."

Yes I say I'm crazy raving drunk. I'm ex-Marine.

"Are you all right?" he says. "Is there anything I can do?"

I have no answer.

I place the talking bone in its cradle.
It has finally said what I needed to hear. I fall asleep.

Telephoning Ginsberg

For Charles Plymell

"Charley said I should call,"
I told him.
"I don't have time to see my own mother.
Why see you?" he answered.

"But if Charley says so, OK,
2:30 tomorrow afternoon,
Lower East Side."

Tomorrow came
and so did the movers
a day early. A small wiry man
driving a semi from Alabama.

"This here New York City?" he blurted.

"Yes," I answered,
the Empire State building framed in
The window behind me.

"That street down there safe?" he asked.
"Yes," I said.
"My ten year old's down there.
Ain't nobody going to mess with him is they?"
"No," I said. "I don't think so."

"I know damn well they ain't," he snapped,
"'cause he's got a 45 pistol stuck down his britches."

Then he started in the living room
taking the paintings down
while I called Ginsberg
to tell him I couldn't make it.

"That's OK," he said.
"I don't have time to see my own mother
and I'm packing for the Orient. Let's
just talk over the phone."
Which we did. Until
everything in my apartment disappeared,

leaving me in an empty room
sitting in the Lotus position
talking with Ginsberg while

everything I owned
was in the hands of a child with a gun
and his father, who was probably
pulling into a truckstop in New Jersey,
screaming, "Is this here America? You think
anybody gonna mess with my boy? No they ain't
And I'll tell you why. . . ."

Lost Keys, Coffee and Guns

Just when I've been making big plans to fix someone, anyone
a cup of coffee, I've locked myself out. Starting up to
the fourth floor where my Jinx Removing-Spiritual Power Candle
lights the window.

For weeks I've been planning how I would move into my new place,
light my candle and maybe Steve or Bob would come by
and I would ask domestic things like, "How much sugar? How
much cream?" It would be a kind of house-warming. But instead
I'm locked out.

If Jack's light were shining from the seventh floor, I could
call him. He could let me in. I could sleep on his floor and
get the super to open my door in the morning. Then Jack could
come down and I could offer him a cup of coffee.

The candle is encased in glass covered with decals that say:
run devil run, lucky cat, business, finance, man-woman attraction

In the Brim commercial, the man dressed by L.L. Bean is being
served a cup of instant coffee by his smiling wife to celebrate
the publication of his first short story. An Irish Setter, also
smiling, curls at his feet. I want to be like these people:
inside. I want to be successful like the woman pouring her
brother-in-law a cup of Maxwell House while her sister without
make-up stares at the floor.

I imagine Jack showing up at any moment to open his door:
pouring me a shot of Wild Turkey, opening his gun cabinet, showing
me his exotic military weapons: Soviet machine-gun, Syrian
carbine, automatic French shot-gun, custom made M-14 with sniper
scope—panning it across the skyline. . .

and Jack would say something like, "I don't know why the government
allows people to have things but as long as they do
I might as well."

Then when the super came I could invite Jack down to my place,
Steve would show up, Bob, Carl, Leo. . . Maybe I could even entice
the super in. "Say fellows, how bout a cup of coffee?"

Then when they got up to leave, they would all forget their keys.
My table shining with metal. Then I could say, "I'm not the only one.
I'm not alone."

But instead, I'm locked out. Feeling much the same about
voodoo candles as Jack feels about military weapons. If
the government allows you to have them, why not?

Tomorrow I'm going down to buy the purple John The Conqaroo
house-blessing candle, the yellow Money Drawing candle, the white
Anti-Hexing candle, the red Protection Against All Harm and Evil Candle
that says: *Proteccion Contra Maldad, Envidias Y Peligros*
and underneath: a hooded skull with dice and dagger.

RUN DEVIL RUN

But for now, I'm like the sister with no make-up, wishing I were
inside making coffee for anybody, even myself, and I don't
even like the stuff.

RUN DEVIL RUN

Melanie Jordan

Ghost Season

Hibiscus in January, the only stars
visible, furious blooms just

as the leafless banana trees jag
their way into the Houston air.

Winter evaporates here like alcohol
on a cotton swab, and left is a half

summer which will hang on until
the summer proper starts swinging,

and then on into October, really,
so that fall's caterwaul is all we get:

suppressed, every season but the burning
one. Imagine a world of extremes

loping off with the largest
shares, this near tropical hotbox;

think of laboring to breathe inside
a sauna, a white towel soaking

with your sweat, your pores gorging
themselves like wicks, skin nearly sentient

with stinging heat and wood; think
of the rising blister from a hot skillet

accidentally stuck to skin, and you'll know
how, when she claimed her kiss from you

in front of me, I became both
humiliated autumn and igneous summer,

my ignorance at once slapped awake,
and god, I haven't seen snow in years.

A Mural in the Abandoned Cane Hill Asylum

Someone, a Giotto just learning to turn
angels, pilfered paint from the wards,

arrowed into a pastoral v
a state-approved horizon, trees

flat as tape, sheep cottage-big.
The sky is only blue like this

in mind, as sheep are clouds with legs,
but clouds nonetheless, implying

a wind's cradle, boundless drift.
In riffling heaps, papers warp

in the next room, still-legible
little accountants: they seep

pneumonia, thrombosis, schizophrenia,
each patient's cordwood years,

typed by one of an army of Royal
machines like the one flashing

mute keys, hunched widow
in its mustardseed room.

In Art Therapy, I think, someone
mastered for a common room

a common vision easy as breathing,
as hard to describe as snow evaporating

on a mitten. Someone stenciled
look what they've done to my brain, ma

in rainbow pencils on a page.
All the paint has bubbled and split.

At the top of the wall, before the scene
trucks itself into a door,

a train runs central on a track
like a black beak on a green wing.

It hovers there like a raised arm
on one reclaimed wall, sanctioned

and still bearing down, the locomotive
like a sentence you were asked

not to repeat, like a word
no one wants to hear.

Pat Landreth Keller

Draglines

1.

twins   the ones she told us were murdered
floated through the telling so many times

she believed she saw them dragged to the river's flat surface
that calm spring day   barbed wire for collars

twelve   she said   pretty little girls
tossing slippers and stockings up the sandy bank

tucking hems into their bloomers   wading the shallows
at the cowpath's end   water lapping the willows

barehanded man whipping wire into lassoes
spinning those girls like sugar   tied back to back

2.

shuffling old man   thick-tongued   sad
coins sticky in his open hand
she said he tried to kiss her   she said

she tried not to think of twins two weeks in the water
strung together like beads

silver spilling from his fingers
he said   *closer*
hand under her dress   she said like water rising

she felt his tongue each time
she slipped a hidden nickel from under the shaving soap
her papa left behind   she said if she dropped the nickel

the old man's words rolled under the door
gotta little honey by the stockyard   comes to my room
likes my hand on her   sweet little leg

she said she'd kept the taste of metal
fingerprints on her thigh   old as she was
said the twins never would quit turning in her mind

washing into the river   out of the river
hair tangled in the willows
just like wanting   she said   just like words

The Woman at the Window

From her high window
she can't see the wrinkling,
only the wide, loose sleeves of my skin kimono,
the white marble columns supporting my torso,
the sterling helmet made pewter by water.

The morning I forgot and left the light on,
I walked naked down the hall to the bath,
its shutters left open to the horns of the moon.
I imagined what she must be saying to herself
looking down from her window into my world:

How good it is to be young! with breasts as alert
and welcome as lights kissing the night;
to have the vessel of my body taut and full,
a water-skin at the beginning of a difficult journey,
safe in the arms of a grateful traveler.

Although old and alone, I am at ease in the shower,
suds slowly addressing deep folds and furrows,
as I give over to water all that time has leached and expanded,
though the clouded mirror can't count the islands of the body
or judge how much of the forest has disappeared.

I rose from the mist like a warning from a long, primeval sleep,
never meaning to frighten her.
If I remind her of a beast, let it be a walrus,
serene in the widening net of the lens,
or perhaps a whale,
a creature we all would travel to see, and yearn to hear singing.

Not for Publication

We're on the phone talking about *Poetry*,
his chances of breaking in, and I'm a believer.
This guy is good, solid,
five books out already, but he's saying,
"*Poetry* publishes almost nothing that they get,
and I've been sending poems to them since 1958,
since I was 19, and I'm getting *old*."

Then I remember my friend can't use a computer,
thanks to poverty and chronic pain,
like John McCain can't use a computer because of torture,
so there we are, my friend and I, ironing out the details
of his future *Poetry* submission via me, on my computer,
while I'm thinking my friend, being a liberal,
might not like the comparison, even if McCain is military,
but not a former Marine, like my friend.
On the other hand, a few weeks ago
we heard an English professor say, in twenty years
Roethke would be dropped like a rock from textbooks.
We both breathed sorrow into the summer air;
we both felt tortured, though I not physically.

My friend, though, suffers every day,
so I had meant to tell him about my father,
who had suffered in a different way,
in the Merchant Marine in the Arctic,
at the wheel of his ship after a torpedo attack.
Another ship had gone down. Dad was turning his ship
to avoid the wreckage, and the waters were awash
with arms and legs, and blood and ice,
and he couldn't change his course or slow the ship
to try to save all those men in the water.
Then the screaming stopped, and the men sank,
but the ships' engines never quit turning
as the convoy, unarmed, tried to run for it,
unable to throw out lifelines, not knowing
when or where the submarines might fire again;
besides, my father said, he didn't want to get hit, sink,
and be chopped up, didn't want to hear
any more sailors screaming, or more of them to realize
they were about to be ground to chum by a giant propeller,
because he knew he would hear them exponentially in his sleep, forever.

But there are other forms of torment,
one my friend can tell you about at age sixty-
seven—bone spurs like tiny needles piercing his lungs,
pains in every joint and never enough medication,
abusive parents, uncaring wives, and animals mistreated.
Not to mention that perennial, universal serpent's tooth.
He can tell you about Roethke, in every anthology, a child
standing on top of a greenhouse with everybody looking up at him
(the way some of us still do), a poet loving life as much as the sailors,
the officers, the men firing torpedoes, and the men bleeding
from separate halves into the water, who loved life
more attentively than the people wanting to chop Roethke out of books.

If my friend were on watch, and a cargo of books entered his waters,
and Roethke weren't in them, he'd blow that ship out of the water,
and if the editors got chewed up by the propeller, and the publishers,
especially, he would just keep circling until they were all gone,
and those of us left would get together at the Old Folks'
Kulture Klub and hoist our beers and throw out lines
from Roethke and other dead poets about to be kicked off the page
on their way to that fate worse than death, oblivion.

For the rest of our lives, we'd man our guns,
the birds soft-sighing above us;
our battle cry, "Snail, glister me forward!,"
the barrel aimed at Academe.
The only thing is, we are getting old, *are* old,
and have not even gotten into the pages of *Poetry*
and I, at least, have few or no prospects.
In fact, we have no control over anything once we step off
the planet, a direction we are hobbling toward
faster than we like to think.
We will already have gone over the edge
when Roethke is cut loose, we hope,
so we won't have to suffer more than we're suffering now,
which is too much, just thinking about him, a great poet,
who after all is just one canary in the mine,
or, as my father would say, just one sailor in the water.

Now here we are, my friend and I,
still twenty years away from a beloved voice gone silent,
and we are already coming apart,
starting to bleed and bob and go under.
When we first stood on the greenhouse with Roethke,
which of us would've believed
the forces of darkness were already gathering;
were, in fact, trampling the flowers below, barbarians
loading their catapults with brimstone, awaiting the word?

Collin Kelley

The Virgin Mary Appears in a Highway Underpass

Mary pops up in the strangest places,
usually as a window stain or sandwich,
but yesterday she dripped down the wall
of a Chicago underpass, brought the faithful
running with candles and offerings, blocked traffic.
I saw the pictures, couldn't see her face,
saw a giant, gaping vagina instead, just failed
my Rorschach Test, going to hell for sure.

If this is Mary, she sure gets around,
recasting herself as a Holly Golightly,
popping up where you least expect her,
causing trouble for the locals.
Buy why would she choose to appear
in condensation, burnt toast or ditch water runoff?
Some will say it's proof that she still dwells here,
runs like an undercurrent, manifests in the mundane.

I say, cut the parlor tricks, Mary.
If you want a little respect, come flaming
out of the sky on a thunder cloud,
ride it like a magic carpet over Middle America,
speak in a voice like Diana Rigg or Emma Thompson,
command attention instead of this sleight of hand,
a stain to be cleaned with soap and water,
so easily erased.

Three Mile Island

I still dream of those snowy white smokestacks,
permanent mushroom clouds.
The way the news cameras caught them in the flaming
sunrise over the Susquehanna. It was late March
but when I remember the meltdown, it seems like summer.
Maybe it was that fear of being cooked or the earth
opening up and sinking us all to China.
I wanted to be there, wearing plaid pants, wide collar
jacket and my dad's Vitalis slicking back my hair.
Wanted that microphone, puffed like cotton candy,
against my lips in near hysteria at the scoop of 1979.
I couldn't sleep for five days, waiting for the hydrogen
bubble to burst and kill us all. Pennsylvania seemed
really close when I was 10 and the doomsday mass
held by the Harrisburg priest didn't help. He offered
general absolution and I, not even a Catholic,
not having yet set foot in a church, quietly prayed
to be a witness, an Armageddon altar boy.
In school they used to make you crawl under a desk
with your hands locked over your head, as if this could
save you from the bomb. Fuck that.
If I'm going to be incinerated, I don't want the slow
leaching death of cancer. I want to be standing
at the window as the flash comes, like those soldiers
at Trinity 1945, sunglasses reflecting a fire that should
have never been conjured, the wind in my hair.

Anthony Kellman

Early Birds

Pre-dawn darkness.
Mockingbirds, loud, happy,
fastened to the morning like grommets.
Two older women with cane lances
walk slowly in conversation.
A group of shirtless men
run and talk. A young woman jogs
alone and unafraid.
Two blossoming dogwoods
suddenly rise softly from a lawn
like Civil War ghosts guarding the red-brick columns
that are stitched with ivy sutures.
The moon's a half wafer on God's lips
over Arsenal and Walton Way, over
the earth-compacted dead.
Hooded and panting, I inhale
cool air as yet untarnished
by the day's exhausts. I move
with my own particular ease,
my own particular joy, alone
but not lonely, finding
some merited peace
in exile's daily course.

Epiphany Through a Small Town

. . . A garbage can brimming with last week's leavings.
A Baptist graveyard with fresh-cupped flowers.
A canal full with recent rain. Glazed
with indifference, a pertly flowering magnolia.
Past the dollar store and small-town Farmer's Bank,
a family of six approach the bus; one,
a Nike-clad youth, baseball cap on backwards, headphones
clasping his head, hitches baggy jeans drooping below white boxers.
Two of the women break ranks, hug and kiss
the arrivants, then wait in waving merriment
in the Tyre Center lot. PRAISE HIM shouts
from the front of a cerulean T-shirt.
In the distance, a phalanx of forty-foot pines.
Woodstacks. Sunlight over a meadow, green from
last week's rain. Sweet sunlight over pasturing cows.
Silent black cows. Sweet silent sunlight.
Land For Sale. Five to Fifty Acre Lots.
Baby pine groves delicate and fragile as life.
Whenever we manage to become intimate, you spoil it.
You get authoritarian, as if you own me. It was. . .
it was so long ago I forget when we last made love.
I don't think we'll ever make love again.
It's best this way, to live conveniently—Someone mows the lawn,
pays the bills, takes out the garbage. Someone cooks, washes,
buys groceries. Fine. As if summoned, rain clouds
close in like an overpass. Then, as suddenly, light
softens on adult pines. Storage For Rent.
Baby pines stretch for miles like rows of rattooned
sugar cane, the hard mauve stalks waving,
sweet in maturation, but calloused
and burdened within each self-protecting carapace.

Bill King

Crow Addresses the Mythmakers

Why does crow pick to pieces squirrel's nest?
Don't say *It's his nature, bird of black intent,*
harbinger of death or bane, bother, pest.

My most raucous caw cries a most urgent request:
I am blackest black on bluest blue, not rent
by thirst, outcast. Look hard. Who first guessed,

watching me lift without sound, without jest,
that I wove dark threads through fog meant
to stitch shrouds for each and each and each? Lest

you forget, on whose order, on what divine behest
were you moved to crow what you have pent
all season? What do you mean, croaking without rest?

Do you a fig in your throat you can't digest?
Why not stop confessing and repent—
hush and lift; sew your own black thread west.

Your caw is a curse best not blessed.
Why not stop confessing and repent—
hush and lift; sew your own black thread west.
What do you mean? What do you mean croaking without rest?

The Pond

Because two horses
lifted their heads beneath
an apple tree at the top of the hill
and snorted

I waded across the creek
slipped beneath the barbed wire
that stitched the hem
of old man Warner's field

and rowed my arms through
late summer grass
before stepping out of the field
and into the rut on the other side
the horses had made to gorge on
sweet green apples spotted with mold

It was from beneath the apple tree
that I first saw old man Warner's pond
pushing clouds along the earth
and that is when I first saw everything
that was between here and there

the smell of clover and carrion
the snap of grasshopper wings
the sudden cross of a redtail blown sideways
and circling, watching everything below
even the bullfrogs flopping and turtles sliding
into dark water

I walked full round twice
not knowing what I had found
nor that this was the first of a thousand future leavings
of which I still can never tell anyone
where or why I am going

David King

Dusk at the Starlight Drive-In

The ghost of James Dean walks tonight,
Watches us brave the bad neighborhood,
Enter the gravel drive that winds
Through a field lit with bug lights,
Come to the screens.
We tune our dials to AM radio 530,
And on frequencies once held captive
By pulpit pounding Baptists,
Await the beginning of another ritual.
There is no respect for the old movie
Condemned to play again
For a slowly undressing audience.
Our awe lies instead with the moon
That will come upon us like another age,
When shadows held no refuge for bums,
And the air did not reek of cheap liquor.
Some things have remained as always—
The rolling bruise of thunder clouds,
Gravel dust stirring under
The slow crunch of tires,
Fogged rear windows closing
On the smell of stale popcorn.
We come here always as children,
Perhaps to the place of our conception,
Certain of the power in the red sun falling,
And the redemption present
In a thousand flickering images,
The stars giving rise to new light.

Night Trains

Coming out of Winder, Georgia,
Careening down U.S. Highway 29,
You may hear them,
And if you are lucky enough
To survive the two-lane that rips
Through the towns like a wound,
You can ride alongside them,
All the way to the interstate.
When I get near the spark singing wheels,
I roll down all the windows,
Turn off the radio, let the bellowing
Music of steel and a diesel engine
Take me the rest of the way.
The engineer seems the only one left alive.
I wave for him, hit the high beams,
Listen for my yells echoing
Through cemeteries, front porches,
Yards of whitewashed Baptist churches.
Eventually I lose them around a curve
Where the road and tracks split away.
The locomotives lunge and barrel
Into a damp tunnel of kudzu.
On the trestle over the river,
I hear one last wail,
A final howling of brakes to the rails,
A fading rumble as the trains clear the bridge,
And we ride together at night,
Right off the edge of the world.

Hilary King

I Do Not Have Mary Oliver's Apple Tree

Or her fox, that speaks so plainly and beautifully
about how death is a kind of music.

I do have a bucket from Wal-mart.

Sky blue, with a high arch of a handle
and a low, round well for holding,
it was made for Easter.
Yellow chicks dance on its sides.

The bucket has lasted past
the sunrise of babyhood
through the too hot morning
of early boyhood
to sit now by the driveway,
holding rain-softened sticks
of colored chalk,
my son's reach for it
routine and extraordinary
as any orchard's tree.

Alyse Knorr

Alice Recalls Georgia to Jenny

Let me show you the forests submerged in kudzu waist-deep,
the red clay of the riverbed that would stain our hands and fingertips,
or Dock J of the Bald Ridge Marina, where I first fell in love
with a woman when I saw her weeping.

Inside the old revival shacks, grass grows through the boards year-round.
I pass them and remember the story from grade school: a summer night,
june bugs fatter that year than ever, and two girls crashed their pickup
on Campground Road and died.

Give me your hand; I will lick away the orange in the paths of your palms
and we can find a road where I might still be waiting,
among the green growing higher and higher.

Robert Krut

Walking Toward the Blue Song

The flashlight looks over
the engine, the raised hood, the oil on my palms.
Beyond this shoulder is a hill, dark green
from night time, and small box of a church.

It could be a crate from this distance, no ornaments
other than the sign proclaiming *First Signs of God*.
The flashlight's arm stretches
up the hill and tugs my wrist.

I wake the caretaker inside. He speaks
in sleeptalk—sliding apart
in the middle of syllables. It is
indecipherable, and I think

this is a house for faith, for snake handlers
speaking in tongues. While he talks, I can see
his hands raised, copperhead pivoting in his palms,
his legs bouncing, voice gaining momentum.

He nods and leads me back behind the altar, through
an oak wood door and into a corridor—long,
hidden. Mirrors cover the walls, and behind
the mirrors, rustling. The glass reflects itself, amplifies sound.

We stop. There is a band
at the other end, behind a scrim, their music
hard to hear. Distant country blues
through gauze, humming through a pinhole in the night.

Their bodies are far, and coated with the hall's only light, blue—
fire blue, pilot light blue—
their skins are blue and translucent like a flame,
blue flame without an eye.

I am afraid to go there. The caretaker knows, speaks
in my ear, crisp now—

yes, they are . . . and I know he wants me
to walk to them, but I am afraid—

in the mirrors, my profile
steps further down. Outside,
it is so black, and here
I can feel the heat of their skins, song.

Being Somewhere I Shouldn't

I swear the moon isn't a moon—
it's eye without iris, it's an eye

watching me stand at your door.
When I blink, that eye blinks with me.

I pause, know you are inside, writing
the words to a song on the radio.

Pressing the doorbell, sound stretches, diameter
growing until it surrounds my feet, my head—

I lean into its vortex, windwarped black.
Breathe deeply. Pulling back, the circle

shrinks down to the hole on a guitar
your palm across the strings—

speak to me about the inside of earth
and how I'm there with you.

Strum the guitar, the circle grows again.
The notes ring and echo and fade

on the porch, opening to your eyes
when you see my face and say, I'm here.

Joshua Lavender

The Death of Auntie Bellum's Attic

It begins with soft plinks
on a mirror propped in the dark.
In rivulets water snakes down
the basement's ancient brick wall
and puddles under an old sofa,
plotting a washout of rummage.

The town's scrapbooks are scattered
across these shelves, companions
to Zane Grey novels grandfathers read,
cigar boxes, coke bottles, Clue sets,
coin collections, rings, trinkets
passed from mother to daughter.

The water rises, makes its presence
                felt. A tide jostles crates
of Perry Como and Lawrence Welk.
A mannequin flails and drowns.
Joists rotten from age and neglect
at last collapse, and with a groan a world
of water crashes in, hoists furniture—
wicker chairs, chaise lounges, trunks—
everything flounders in a sea of blackness.

Insatiable, the water crawls up creaking stairs
to claim a kingdom of gleaming junk.

The story's facts, the wistful obituary
in the Union-Recorder, end there,
but still, in images that flash
between their days and acts,
the people see water slinking
into their basements, flooding
the flotsam of their lives.

It starts its creep upstairs.

And the drenched dawn finds them
huddled on rooftops with suitcases,
urns, their children and their old
gathered under tattered blankets.

They gaze at their town, now a lake.
With hesitant, unversed lips they pray
for rescue, refugees from what began
as only weeping.

Kathleen Brewin Lewis

Whereupon the Writer Thinks She is the Center of the Universe

In a lonely corner of the night,
she sits writing at the kitchen table
while her house sleeps.
But the outside is trying to come in.
Dusty moths and brown beetles
are beating on the glass,
covering the window panes with
their soft wings and crisp bodies,
drawn to, absolutely craving,
her light.
She is spooked, distracted,
she is finally flattered,
writing more intently
for her fluttering audience,
strangely moved
by the staccato of their gentle collisions.
This night is alive, she is thinking,
It is pulsing with the beat of my heart.
And all eyes—
All of the tiny, glittering eyes—
Are on me.

Cody Lumpkin

Cooking Spam Outdoors

I slice the Spam, thick as a wad
of cash, with a pocket knife
I just bought. Then drop the jellied flesh
into an aluminum skillet and wait

for the sizzle to drown out the endless
throat-clearing of the cheap propane
stove. The mule deer in the vacant
field of the KOA campground mock

us with their twitching ears, their shit-
pellets strewn like buckshot over every
square foot. To them, we are scarcely better
than the gassy, snorting bovines on the other side

of the barbwire fence. The deer leap from one
side of the prickly parallel lines to the other,
while we have trouble balancing
on the picnic table and must sit across

from each other as if in a restaurant,
waiting for the Spam to blacken and crisp.
I turn the meat with a small spatula purchased
from the pricey camp store. We have driven

across several states and crossed major
American rivers, a three coffee break drive,
to eat Spam here. A distance that took
white folks months to cross in prairie

schooners, the unfit dying along the long
imperceptible, uphill trudge. Devils Tower,
bulbous, cinematic looms like a hunk
of Spam beset by a toddler with a spork.

Its rust red rock browns in the gloaming
against a sky that begins to spark with stars.
The night is a greasy cast iron pan. We wave
our slivers of dinner in the air, then nibble.

168

Squirrel Metaphysics

When you and your mother live
in a house on stilts in the deciduous
forests of Georgia, and she leaves
an open bucket of bird seed where
the foundation never was, you will
get visitors, grey ones with tails
that follow them to the next tree
over trickling creeks, across yellow-veined
asphalt by-ways.

                        One summer, a squirrel
fell into the millet and chaff. The scooper
cupped him perfectly, a see-thru cage,
a curious experiment gone wrong.
The bird seed was quicksand
up to his small white chest. Even after
my mother and I climbed down the steps
to see what made the crackling racket,
the squirrel never stopped biting
the hard plastic trap that encircled him.
Animals have no shame.
They only think of living. His cheeks
stained with dark red blood, jaw mouthing
a way toward freedom.

                        When my mother
finally lifted the handle out of bucket,
the only sounds left were the rustle of leaves,
the tap of claws on a nearby oak.

Thomas Lux

Refrigerator, 1957

More like a vault—you pull the handle out
and on the shelves: not a lot,
and what there is (a boiled potato
in a bag, a chicken carcass
under foil) looking dispirited,
drained, mugged. This is not
a place to go in hope or hunger.
But, just to the right of the middle
of the middle door shelf, on fire, a lit-from-within red,
heart red, sexual red, wet neon red,
shining red in their liquid, exotic
aloof, slumming
in such company: a jar
of maraschino cherries. Three-quarters
full, fiery globes, like strippers
at a church social. Maraschino cherries, maraschino,
the only foreign word I knew. Not once
did I see these cherries employed: not
in a drink, nor on top
of a glob of ice cream,
or just pop one in your mouth. Not once.
The same jar there through an entire
childhood of dull dinners—bald meat,
pocked peas and, see above,
boiled potatoes. Maybe
they came over from the old country,
family heirlooms, or were status symbols
bought with a piece of the first paycheck
from a sweatshop,
which beat the pig farm in Bohemia,
handed down from my grandparents
to my parents
to be someday mine,
then my child's?
They were beautiful
and, if I never ate one,
it was because I knew it might be missed
or because I knew it would not be replaced
and because you do not eat
that which rips your heart with joy.

Beneath the Apple Branches Bent Dumbly

Beneath the apple branches bent dumbly
with the blank weight of their blossoms—
the grass and me—completely
alive with one thought
like a shin struck with an axe: What
is the same each summer? I know
that the ring of cold slung
through my chest grows colder, that the mountains'
lowly crags grow imperceptibly rounder, but what
is the same? Not the driveway
littered (in a few months) with crushed
apples swarmed by yellowjackets—those cruel
insects, not the hackneyed
rock garden, its pool for goldfish
long filled in with dirt and a few
ill-bred petunias, not the heat bugs
and their high whine . . . . What
is the *same*? Only the incomparable chins
of horses, only a desire
to place the mural of a pond
horizontal as it belongs,
only the long haul in the linear world, ongoing.

There Were Some Summers

There were some summers
like this: The blue barn steaming,
some cowbirds dozing with their heads
on each other's shoulders, the electric fences
humming low in the mid-August heat. . . .
So calm the slow sweat existing
in half-fictive memory: a boy
wandering from house, to hayloft, to coop,
past a dump where a saddle rots
on a sawhorse, through the still forest
of a cornfield, to a pasture talking to himself
or the bored, baleful Holsteins nodding
beneath the round shape of a catalpa, the boy
walking his trail toward the brook
in a deep but mediocre gully,
through skunk cabbage and popweed,
down sandbanks (a descending
quarter acre Sahara), the boy wandering
thinking nothing, thinking: Sweatbox,
sweatbox, the boy on his way
toward a minnow whose slight beard
tells the subtleties of the current, holding there,
its water cold enough to break your ankles.

Dan Marshall

Koan

Like a beautiful impenetrable koan the words wind themselves around your heart, like smoky music in some Saturday night sweatbox bar, but it's not music when you hear it because you don't hear it really; you shout over it, never realizing how hoarse you sound until between songs. But when you finally step outside into the air (and it's always cool outside), your pockets full of wet change and your eyes watering as you blink in the cold and your head clears and with every move your head starts to loll as the ghost in the machine drives you down country roads, gray and clear in the moonlight. The windows are down and the cold air rushes in. Outside it is just air, but you by your motion make it a wind. And the wind forms out of itself long, beautiful, impenetrable questions.

Christopher Martin

Antidote to Narcissus

—for Erik Reece

I've heard the great blue heron
cannot see its own reflection
cast from the water's surface—

a gift that it may never lose a fish
in the image of a perfect eye
or fail to see a frog amid
such slate feathers shed
from a rookery on high.

If only we could fade that way
into the mist of rivers,
into rhododendron shade;

if only we could be so beautiful
and not know a thing about it.

Revelation on the Cherokee County Line

At an exit off I-75, a coyote rots on the ramp,
green, not with fierce fire, but with fungus, mold
embalming its bloated body, its once black hair.
Its face looks up from itself, a monster
petrified on concrete, teeth still bared.
Above this flesh a sign says *Tourist Info*,
arrow points west, past the Wendy's.
What more information would they need
to tell them they are not here, but anywhere?

James May

Natural Grief

To see the four crows surrounding the fifth,
the sick one, this morning and all afternoon
as it died on our driveway, leaving its carcass
and a smattering of sun-dried feces—to see them stay
until one nudged the dead with its beak
and, receiving no response, paused for a moment,
a long moment, before taking a full and what looked like
exaggerated stroke of its wingspan that lifted it away,
an action the others followed. To see
that long vigil through casual and then more frequent returns
to the kitchen window and not think the birds
feel something comparable to our sorrow
would be, I think, a dismissive mistake. Like the phrase
bearable tragedy. Or the condolence Well, he lived
a long life. . . I kept hearing at my grandfather's wake,
in the same tone you'd use to justify a bad
but free meal. Three days ago, our neighbor, Jane,
an eight year-old adopted as an infant from China,
told us she was getting a baby sister, and yesterday,
her arms around our dog, she told my wife
that she and her parents weren't going to China again,
that something went wrong, that her sister's blood test
wasn't right, something she didn't understand.
It's weird, she said, to be sad about someone you haven't met.
Jane was left outside a hospital on a snowy night
in December, wrapped in blankets. Her birth parents
cared enough to make sure she'd be found.
The crow seemed to weigh less than the bag
I shoveled it into. When she saw me
place it all in the garbage can on the curb, Jane asked
what it was, and I lied. And then told her the truth.

The Reddened Flower, the Erotic Bird

Out running one morning in early October, at the top of a hill,
I found myself ten feet from an owl perched on a fencepost.

In its beak, a thick cord of taut tissue still attached to the squirrel,
which twitched beneath the talons until the owl, seeing me, dropped it—

and we stood, staring at each other through the cold, barely lit air.
I have told this so many times, but no one, I understand, will understand

the original rapture (yes, I'll use that word) of that moment.
Do we report stories like these—my mother calling me

to say she and my father saw a white ("not an albino!
It had brown eyes") deer in their yard; or Chelsea, almost breathless,

keys still in her hand, describing the sprinting shadow of the coyote
she may or may not have seen but is pretty sure she had

near the train tracks less than a mile from our house—
do we report them because they are stand-ins, almost,

for grace? And what cynicism keeps me from saying
that we do so because we love, and are surprised by, the world?

Fringe Tree

–Or Old Man's Beard.

That the names we give recall the thing
is what we want. And yet, both names are boring
when compared to the way it shimmers there
like a firework that somehow doesn't fall,
or the way it will fall eventually
from itself, swirling its gauzy pollen
in the wind above the lawn
where the children next door run outside in late April,
swearing to their mother that it's snowing.
And even after they know they're wrong,
they squeal, insisting their mistake
is something to dance through, something
to repeat and repeat again—not hoping
to make it right, just enjoying what it is
and what it looks like the more they say so.

mariana mcdonald

Father's Day, Lake Pontchartrain

–for MAJ

Boats on the lake. Boats on the lake.
At water's edge the young boys make great circles
with the rocks they throw in the water,
while toe to toe the skaters peel
along the shores.

Men and their sons. Dads and their girls.
At levee's edge a raucous whirl of laughter
weaves the air with shrieks,
the language happy boyhood speaks,
and bounces off the passing belch of motorcars.

Father's Day, Lake Pontchartrain.
At evening's edge the orphans and the childless
stay parked in their cars,
while even the newly fatherless
boundless play with the stars,
as they breathe the certain rhythm of the waves.

Sandra Meek

Acacia karroo Hayne (White Thorn)

Ivory monastery, you invite
retreat, your quills without ink, your needles
hollow; you are slow exhalations
of whistled breath, both cut
and seam, the noteless stems of music a girl
scores into her arms; you are the soul's
razored canister. Antennae
of many voices, you tune to the milky ships
of distant planets, your fray of ghosts
without waists, without wrists, a crystalline heart
slivered to fossil trails
of shooting stars; you are the desert's
drained hourglass, its whittled
vanishing, you are the bristling unlit incense of fog
and sea-froth, your liver-spotted sleeves
the stiff papery threads
of a petrified fountain, village cookfires' lingering veil
honed to narrow vials, to spines of moonlight
echoing the body's
deepest wands, the cuneiform
of longing, how you avoided pain
by becoming its measure, your starved scepters clinging
to anyone passing.

Coma

How the body, suspended, becomes memorial
to what it used to house: wooden cross
starring the roadside; silver jet trail
expanding as it fades, underscoring then canceling the clouds'
inscrutable calligraphy. There is no shared language
between us and the night. When the truck
struck the convertible's side and sent us reeling
through oncoming cars, glinting waves
miraculously parting, what say did I have
over the words flung from me? As if I
broke to nothing but the teleology
of circumstance, flotsam of whatever random
predestination traffics with us, tipping the scales

so we come up *yes*, and she,
no—Tell me, as you wait
in your mother's hospital room
gone too dark to separate shadow
from body, while in the hall they debate
the ethics of respirators, of splitting the chest
to press that beat back into the hypothetically
stalled heart, where was she, as the scan
inked mourning around the brain's
one lit wing? What sound does the soul make
leaving the body? And how distinguish it
from the machine's pump and sigh, from steel
crashing against steel? But we walked

away from our wreck, days before the call
that she'd been hit; wobbly as new fawns
on the highway shoulder, grit of gravel like ground
eggshell beneath our feet, in that moment
nothing mattered, not whether we'd been targeted, spared,
overlooked, next to the crystal of broken bottle necks,
beer cans' silver spillage shimmering
in the ravine's long grass. As if that lovely green
wasn't our vision of this earth
already fraying. As if living
each day in the warmth of what would blind
if directly faced, we could keep from turning
to that brilliant, unforgiving knowledge, that the light

has never revolved around us, despite our picturing the sun
as a daily, gifted gesture. On southern
highways, styrofoam crosses mark where car
hit tree: loss hammered to a precise station,
like the one floret pricked red at the center
of Queen Anne's Lace, those stiff umbels of foam lining
the shoulder, as if in each heart the compass foot dug
too deeply in. What's a circle but a line
that can't let go? The names are what's blurred
at 65 miles per hour, and everything said is a radius spun
away from that point everything
points to, when the machine is turned off and she
breathes, or doesn't, with whatever's left of what we'd

call her will. The last of the late
afternoon light blows through the pines edging
the highway. Any two points
on a circle form an arc: directionless, and so
eternal. But the sun's dropping behind the horizon
of her window; the linear keeps breaking
through the visible world, denying the consolation of the whorls
you keep rubbing into her palm as her heart flickers
on the monitor. No comfort left, only
this: What took her breath
wasn't yours given back, what tonight you'd give
not to see her heart's handful of electric dust
falling in line across that screen.

Tillandsia Usneoides

You could walk under it your whole life
and never know it flowers, magnolia's waxy moons
eclipsing the blooms, never know
it houses chiggers, red flecks

of dormant fire. Spanish moss,
graybeard, thrives on fences, telephone
wires, winds cemetery oaks
with cursive scrawls weeping

over block letters in stone.
Don't we want to believe in living
without the machinery of life,
holding our breath through eternity

at the bottom of the pool,
unending time to make over each flailing
fluid gesture to sign language's
precise fluency? Science the art

of elaborate misnaming, it's not a moss
but an herb, related to the pineapple, as Irish moss
is an alga, reindeer moss a lichen, and the air fern's
not a plant at all but an oceanic skeleton,

dyed green. What we make
in the image of this world, is it art
or description's drapery: Christmas tinsel stripped
of silver to essence, shredded

copperish paper; not a sachet of hair
rescued from a lost beloved's
ivory brush, its unraveling
nest's composed of a single

living thread which in the end
kills nothing—not a parasite, but merely
a plant living on air, so weightless it resists
gravity, the curious hand's

loving destruction. The ephemeral's
part of the illusion, part of nature's art
beyond our dreamed-up uses—packing material,
upholstery stuffing, the fertility doll's

approximate flesh winding the flowering skirt's
hidden stem: a muse for artifice, its soft
embellished spine. Each loop
leads through the next, a wad of ancient

fishing line marooned in these trees during some
archetypal flood. How easily the moment walking beneath
ravels into forever, the way this sidewalk followed
far enough would end in ocean coral reefs'

chromatic alphabet in endless revision, cobalt
to cream; plankton's pulsing
phosphorescent stars; the fathomless language of whales
we hear as music.

Judson Mitcham

Night

My wife's down the hall, already in bed.
I have dozed off
here in my recliner, the TV bright but mute.
I struggle up to make my little tour.
I check the locks and turn off the lights,
but at the computer, I take a seat.
My son holds his daughter in the photo.
She's eight months old.
Both meet my eyes evenly, as if to say,
"Only the straight truth now, old man,"
and I can't move. In my son's face,
I see love. Forgive me. I see time. I do.
But in hers—
world that was, world that is, world to come.
The screensaver times on, a field of stars,
and I am traveling, as though on a spacecraft
or a planet, but alone, out into the night.
Then, like I'm God,
I move my hand, and there they are again.

Praise

When I heard the learn'd astronomer,
I realized I'd walked into the wrong lecture, so I left

and wandered the halls, finally asked someone
for the right room. And there it was, the wilderness,

already on the screen when I sat down. Hallelujah
for the ions, messiahs out of never. Let the species

say Amen. Let every human
give praise to the membrane, the delicate skin

of the spirit. And to the stars, yes, forever out there,
but we are here, still, in our only time,

humbled by our own cells, our little travels, our
Easters of each day. We are the very

electrons of the uncanny. We are the liquid, tricky
beats that we can't keep up with. Salt of love,

O little thought,
how excellent you are, slowed down, here in the dark.

Tennessee

But there will come a time
when the jar out there on the hill says nothing at all,

when the jelly jar, scoured of every sweet molecule,
or the widemouth pickle jar, words pressed into its side,

lies there as wild
as the blind salamander that crawls all over it,

and whatever those words once said,
they can say that no more. Take the plain Mason jar

delivered to my father's table the year he died.
Or take the headstone engraved with 1989.

Take the grave itself, any grave, or the road, or the sky.
There will come a time when each of these

has no way at all
to mean. There will be no Tennessee. Say a house

settles and creaks, as if set adrift.
It will hold no sadness. In that wild place, there will be

no wilderness.

Maren O. Mitchell

The Sensual Art of Tomato Slicing

Approach expectantly with a thin blade,
serrated, pointed,
long enough to cross the body.
Take your time.
The tomato, succulent salvation of sandwiches,
useable from skin through flesh to seeds,
will tell you where to cut.
No need to chisel, freeing the sculpture within.
Let the knife descend unerringly.
Slices fall upon one another,
wet velvet bound by circular selvage.
Leave nothing. Capture
the escaped liquid and imbibe
the promise of pleasure to come.

Janice Townley Moore

Evening Out

Atlanta, 1952

On days too hot for breath to be easy
my father left his desk in the cellar
to drive our Easter ducks, full grown,
to Piedmont Park for a swim.
Crated up in the trunk of our pea-green Plymouth,
they quaked and quacked the long three miles.
Our whole family went along for the show.
Without coat and tie my father sprawled
in the cool by the lake. I remember
how his wallet bulged in his back pocket
as he bent to unlatch the crate.
No pounding joggers then, only walkers slow as July
and a few children ringing the bells on their bikes.
A quiet crowd inched forward to see the ducks
gliding over the dark reflections of magnolias,
sometimes flapping their wings
with the sound of sheets in the wind.
After paddling among the fallen petals,
they shored up for recrating,
lured by lettuce, as I watched
the late sun glinting off my father's black shoes
sinking into the red clay bank.

Teaching the Robins

If it's true what the Chinese say,
souls can filter into birds like these
two robins outside my window,
swooping down. Their feet land
on March's early green
at the same moment I am teaching
Emily Dickinson's grief,
my throat more taut from last year's losses
than the students slumped,
sleeping under lowered brims
of their baseball caps.
The robins stare in at me. They listen
to my voice hobbling over "tombs,"
"the feet mechanical." They watch me
pacing forth and back behind the panes.
The students sleep on in their numbness
where poetry does not exist
in the lighted arena of their dreams.
I think of all the dead,
how they do not have to worry
about being dead. This morning
life is on the other side of the window
where one robin remains
like an eye comprehending me,
long after the other flies.

Note to the King of Green Lawn Service

Your grass fails to intrigue,
programmed as cloned blades—
bermuda or centipede.
No pleasant wild onion reek,
luck of the four-leafed clover.
Where lies the allure of strawberries,
the first tiny hearts we ate
on a dare for their poison?
No ripe boys roll cigars from weeds.
No queens of the May
sit splay-legged, threading clover
stem upon stem for the longest chain.
In your sad sod dandelions remain extinct,
their little parachutes never blown
by children with grass prints on their knees
into the wild green yonder
till our mothers' voices call us in
across the patchwork giving up its light.

Tony Morris

Blue Iris

I'm driving down the street last week
        when a black Mercedes Benz pulls
out of Kool Beanz Cafe' and runs over

a drunk who'd passed out on the gutter's
        edge, only now he's screaming, howling
really, as he rocks from side to side and grips

his thighs, both legs broken below
        the knees, while the Benz speeds around
the corner and disappears in the dark—

so I pull my car into the drive, jump out and run
        to the man, who's screaming and pointing
and saying. . . muthafucker run over

my legs, d'you see that muthafucker run
        over my muthafuckin' legs, and I'm
saying Okay, Okay—I'll run inside

and call for help—but he's yanking my arm
        and yelling and pointing when I look down
into his blood-veined, yellow-rimmed eyes

and see his sapphire-blue iris, deep,
        warm, closing like a shutter, and I flash
back to my daughter's birth, how I fell

into her dark pupils and floated somewhere
        between was and will be, the blue-veined pulse
at her temple pushing blood beneath the milk-smooth

skin, and leaning down to kiss her head I caught
        the whisper of an inner grace in her infant breath
and in that moment all I knew and all I was

and all I would become faded out and folded
        up, and nothing, not the sound of seabirds flying
high above the eastern shore, nor the smell of hay

in summer, nor the color of the fields
        could ever be the same—and now I sit and hug
the fading drunk who leans against my side

and watch the traffic slow and stop as people
        run for help inside, and I wonder if *his* father saw
the future slipping sideways from his sight,

 and if he ever told his son that every day
        and every night is filled with things we'll never know,
and only yesterday, it seems, he saw you stand and walk alone.

Reflectors

I wrestled with the question for a minute,
    stepped into the cab and leaned against the leather
        as the driver from the wrecker service pulled the chain
beneath the chassis of the crushed and twisted Nova,
    kicking to the shoulder what was left: a chromed
        rear bumper, flakes of paint and rubber smudged
against the silver surface that the owner, maybe yesterday,
    had rubbed and buffed with compound till it shined
        like polished water on a slow, still, humid day
when even high up in the trees the hawks
    are settled in, the only sound a low and level
        rhythm of cicadas as the day is closing down;
a smashed and broken windshield, tinted surface
    crisscrossed in a web of matted glass and plastic
        like a wrinkled, painted hide rolled up and waiting
to be cured; and several shards of busted
    taillight blinking red and yellow in the sun—
        and while the cars lined up behind us, snaking
down along the ridge, I thought about the small,
    red, plastic cowboy boot, a drinking cup
        I'd used when I was young and I'd been riding
many hours in the floor-pan of our coupe,
    half-asleep, or maybe not, because I know
        I found the yellow bottle Dad would squeeze
to fill his lighter tucked beneath the seat
    and somehow opened up the top, poured
        it slowly in the boot, then held the cup up to my lips
and swallowed what I could before the world around
    me stopped—I couldn't breathe, I couldn't talk
        my throat and lungs and eyes all burned,
but I must've coughed or wheezed
    because my mother started screaming
        and my Dad pulled off the road, lifted
me into his arms, then ran up to a farmer's house
    where he and mother yelled and knocked
        until they opened up, and on the phone
the doctor said to feed me milk and keep me still
    and all around the world was gauzy, slow and strange—
        yet nothing ever felt so real—and now I wonder
if the man I just saw roll and flip his car was only scared
    or just confused when he reached, grabbed my arm
        and asked if I were real, or just a dream—so I smiled
and nodded, told him "Yes," then held his hand
    just as my father had, until they slid
        the gurney in the bus, flipped the siren on
and sped away as all along that section
    of the Blue Ridge something glimmered in the sun.

Something about Chickens

The rooster didn't care when mother yanked
the wheel of the red '62 Bonneville, swerved
      into the ditch and smacked against a culvert, back
tire spinning in the red mud as my brother and sister woke
crying from the rear, and Dad leaned back against
      the white vinyl bucket, blood from his busted
nose smeared on his cheek and chin, and I stood up
from behind his seat which he'd pulled forward just enough
      for me to fit into the small dip between the drive-train
and the doorframe, and there the rooster stood, stock still
in the middle of the road, staring, unblinking, indifferent
      as my mother cried and asked if everyone were alright—
and it was 4 a.m. just outside of Sinking Creek, Kentucky were
my grandparents lived, and 1965 seemed the only time
      in the world, and the sun was still an hour from rising,
which it did one hour later when we were all sitting around
the oilcloth covered table in my grandma's kitchen
      and the bare bulb overhead seemed too bright
on Mom's white face—the face I later saw as she lie
if not asleep, then not awake, and silent as that morning
      in '65, since the tumor, now pressed against her left parietal lobe,
caused an aphasia, named after Paul Brocha, French
physician, and anthropologist, lesser known
      for his studies in cancer pathology, who probably also knew,
like president Clinton said about himself, "something about chickens"
since he was raised not in Arkansas, but in Sainte-Foy-la-Grande,
      a fourth century Gallo-Roman villa, frequently visited
by Montaigne (whose witticisms were no help
when faced with a tumor the size of an egg), and also famous for its open-
      square market, where, I'm sure, chickens there knew something
about the chopping blocks, and scratching ground while flinging
headless bodies down those narrow villa streets, their squawking
      heads now silent in the dust, and as my father always said,
find a chicken and a cock's crow won't be far, which might
explain why Mom would never raise a chicken, even after
      she'd retired into the hills to live her last years out—
for as we sat around that table and the sun began to rise,
the rooster raised a shout, and Mom stood up without a word,
      walked outside and wrung the speech right out
of that red rooster, and there both stood—silent
and unblinking at the redness of that early morning sky.

Ginger Murchison

Songwriter

Sometimes, no one singing, no
        window open, a blues thing—
    all by itself, a surprise
at a stoplight, on the back-kitchen stairs—
        oozes, vague-like,
the way neon blinks part of itself in the rain.

Now these three brown envelopes,
        post-marked Savannah: blackbirds
    lifting off pages stained with
all-night nickel coffee, red dirt from the
        two-lanes, and booze—
a life's liquored-up moans from a saxophone's throat.

I'll need cigarettes, chocolate,
        and gin to get through these again:
    songs flung at midnights,
walk that New Orleans and Memphis, the Beats,
        Baudelaire,
the past tense in flickering neon, key of g.

The Orchid

It is spring and I'm full of praise
for every paper-thin petal that pushes its way
out of a deep place, that, like music or color,
makes a brave flare, so I fill the house
and the porches with flowers, most I can't name—
orchids, my favorites, because they are
what art, in the dark, wants to become. One
purple one, the color Crayola calls 39-A,
lasted on my kitchen table for months,
then, its long, naked stalk finally done
with flowering, I tossed it into the compost,
no second thought. Weeks later, audacity
stirred in that pile of rot to come up with four
purple blooms. A ferocious eloquence
I brought back in the house. It isn't breeding.
A simple potato will do the same thing,
hard-wired as it is to play out a belief
in a future it has no word for. Then there's
the cancer that's set up to take over
my sister's lungs—winter, even now,
somewhere, pushing this way.

Guilt

Everything about the South boiling over
            like another consequence
                        in the heaving night air,
rank smell of mildewing magnolia blossoms,
            ripened to rotting, dank end
                        of the blooming season,
cattails like damnation's fingers, moss hanging,
            a tangling, the uncombed beards
                        of father confessors,
and live oaks, bent like arthritic ancestors
            their mock-cover oppressive,
                        each leaf a dry-thirsting
for secrets to whisper along limb to limb
            the hissing song, those long-sighs
                        of night-drawling bird calls,
and me, each breath splintered, even today,
            turning still, every last time,
                        into the wrong ending.

Alicia Rebecca Myers

Insomnia

In the dark your deer shed antlers.
First they hook my ribs with browning tines
until my chest gives, until its chandelier
loosens. My crystalline
swings open your throat the oval
of an unbreakable egg
and for a moment we mirror
our air, we align. Do I lag
behind? I've forgotten myself
like a glove deep in the snow
of you—
     who aren't the wintry shelf
of other men, I know—
but I count restless deer. They leap
the bed, crownless, while you sleep.

Eric Nelson

Fair Road

The sun down but not out,
Houses reduced
To window glow,
Camellias twinkle pink
At the speed of headlights.

In the strip mall more stores
Have closed but one
Like Jesus
Is always coming soon.

It's cold and growing colder, still

The ball fields are filled
With cheer, bright bats
Thwacked, long flies dropping

Like stars at the warning
Track of whatever joy
Can be run down and gloved,

Everyone's hard-to-catch
Breath blasting holes
Into night's falling wall.

The Lowcountry

In our middle age, our parents
Dead and haunting us
As we become more like them,

We live where we couldn't imagine,
The air so wet-heavy and heated
We can barely breathe on land

That was the bottom of a shallow sea
Epochs ago and is still less
Land than water, more trembling earth

Than solid ground, where fortunes grew
In rice and indigo and malaria
Flowed from rivers to families

And nearly the entire city of Savannah,
Its cemeteries so scenic with the dead
They've been designated city parks.

It is difficult to live here, to hold
Firm where nothing holds still,
Where deep roots are impossible

And much we once knew can't live.
Yet much that grows nowhere else
Grows here in this steamy incubator

Where a wild tree thrives
That some call a come tree
For its heavy smell of sex in spring.

In Another Year

All your students will be gone.
No one dropping your name in class,
Reciting you from memory.
None of your bits in their mouths.
In the first year after you died it seemed
Entire classes were yours and I
Was the substitute asking where the chalk is.
The next year they thinned but I knew
Them by their moves, their sudden lunge
For the jugular. Just a few
Remain now and it's mostly by chance
I discover them, like after class
Last week when I saw a sheet on a desk
And thought it was the definitions I'd distributed,
But it turned out to be that Jack Gilbert poem
You gave your classes every semester.
In another year the building will be filled
With students who know you
As a scholarship fund, not you who insisted
They witness everything—including
Your yellowing body those final weeks.
Whenever they wanted explanation
You told them instead to observe
How the man shifts repeatedly the weight
Of the heavy box he carries so that he never
Collapses, but can never put it down.
I don't know if it is grief renewed or
Relief when I see your students disappearing.
I only know that today a dark spear
Streaked toward me on the sidewalk then
Passed through my body like I wasn't there
And when I looked up I had to shield my eyes
To see a hawk pass between me and the sun.

Robert Parham

The Concept of Why

Thump of tires on the old street
underneath like a bad heart,
the white coat man tapping at the laptop,
good at his small talking,
how he's been here all his life,
how the last turn was a good one,
how he's still thinking of something else to do.

Date of birth, he says, goes through the list
I'll hear five more times, the yesses and nos
about diseases, conditions, family history
of things gone bad too soon.

I watch the cars fall back in respect,
give them room to rush me to a place
where I can wait. . . and wait.

Like the next part of a bad dream
I woke from months ago, this starts up,
what waking won't stop. How ER
is not a show on tv, how the huddle
of nurses and technicians calls
not one play but five little ones at once,
leaving the big one for the doctor.

Why did you wait? a senior nurse asks.
I don't know, I lie.

How can I say *Because she died here
almost yesterday?*

Even in places where we pass,
manners are important.

Bed rest: the term a hospital uses
to keep you in one place
but never let you sleep.

People call, others to visit. I give blood
six times a day, then four, then two.
The IV machine goes mad almost hourly,
beeping with the sound from movies
that means someone is dying, his line
gone flat. This one, though, that turns
my blood to water, only wants a rest.

How odd I am here because I stopped
caring, how I had indeed given up,
so goes the reward men get for doing that.
Odd because now I do, a reason found
among the rubble of a life fallen down
about itself. So, I tell me, perhaps
this is it–trapped in the elevator
of my bad health I must smell myself,
hear the ranting in my head yelling
at the only one who deserves it,
at the only one who cares enough
to listen.

                    The ruts in the street
come back at night, whoomp, whoomp,
but like the man with the sonogram
with its whoosh and whoomp, that shows blood
moving, certain parts the clots that move
like chunks of cliff that fall to the river,
begin to move toward the ocean,
that heart of the earth where all things
begin again, where all things stop for good,
where being lost in the world of the blood
gone cold is not a dream at all. Not at all.

The Dark Car Enters

Today the car enters the drive,
a new stranger, black and sleek,
while the day goes white and pale.

The quiet man in a dark suit
gets from behind the wheel to stand
by the door he's closed, to wait.

Mother moves down the entrance
steps while my brother searches
for where she is; I call out

to let him know she's ahead again,
so we need to step up and follow.
We go out and lock the house behind.

I watch the man hold the door
for her, speak and nod, take her arm;
she paused, without words, before ducking in.

"He's not here," she says, to the space
between Ryan and me, so we nod,
assent to our father's absence.

"I mean he's gone, without lingering,"
Mother adds. My brother reaches
for the hand she doesn't offer.

The First Scaffold

Where was the first scaffold,
called something else,
for a different purpose?

The hemp, spun for rope,
was once for something else—
a shirt, a blouse, some pants.

But ropes followed, before chains,
before cable; so, then,
what of the scaffold?

In barns the trap door provides
the place, opened, to drop hay
down for the cow, the horse.

As a farm child I dreamed of it,
the hole in that floor, opening
as I leapt of tall hay, swallowing me.

The hayloft preceded the artist loft,
the pricy loft for living high in city.
On a rail in the ceiling above its floor

hang four large rusty hooks on chains
that drop when released by a rope.
The hooks are pushed into bales of hay,

the bundle lifted high, pulled along rail,
dropped when released at the other end,
dead weight falling to feed another's life.

The barn, dismantled, sold off, the sawed-off
stall of trap door, section of floor, a piece
of the wall, standing, unsold, to itself.

What is that good for? the auctioneer asks.
The crowd, dispersing, spots a pickpocket,
nabs him. "Let's try this," the owner suggests,

finds a rope, tosses it over the stray rafter left
attached to the trap-door gizmo barn piece,
makes a noose, loops, tells the thief to jump.

Amy Pence

8th Grade Locker Combination

If you remember the numbers now,
maybe the rest of your life will click open
on easy street: a winning lottery ticket.

Even then, when it didn't jam,
you considered yourself lucky. Saved
from humiliation, from the dreaded
flicker of girls' eyes
that meant something– .

Yet you didn't think then
that the locker would open
to all these riches: these woods,
this love, this child, even the deaths—
how they come to you in many forms:

wingspans radial, the heron,
the hummingbird: the whir metallic—
approaching, receding again.

Patricia Percival

Beam

The sunflower wears a crown of thorns.
It seeps beams. Bumble bees attend the barn raising.

Barn beams nourish the wood beetles.
A century later, surrounded by suburbs, sun shines

through the roof-lattice. My skirt, your hands.
The fence around the family plot out back.

Root. Roots. A season. A seedling takes
what it needs without apology. The roof,

patched by generations, assumed
by the owl, unmissed by the field mice

for whom walls are enough. They are not safe
from the owl, nor worried, busy with the fallen

sunflowers. The owl calls a summons.
The poet hurries to the dark, the wolf.

They demolish the subdivision.
His arms a scythe of sighs. Her smiles

a fire. The sunflower turns
to the beam, waits for the bee.

Patrick Phillips

Nathaniel

Whatever it was
        that made the Reverend
                Barker stoop that way,

it meant no matter
        how much he screamed
                at my friend Nathaniel

for being late, for not
        raking the leaves,
                or for raking the Goddamned

leaves the wrong Goddamned way,
        he could only ever scowl
                at the tops of his wing-tip shoes

or at the cuffs of the black wool suit
        he always seemed to be wearing
                when he'd thunder into the yard,

or down the stairs, or through
        the little speaker of some payphone
                we huddled around, *God*

damnit Nathaniel, I told you,
        I told you, Nathaniel, Goddamnit!
                his fury repeating

so precisely it became a joke
        we hollered through the halls,
                changing my friend's name

to Goddamnit Nathaniel, as in
        Where the hell's Goddamnit Nathaniel?
                I told you, Goddamnit, to get me a Coke!

which was stupid but funny at fourteen,
      and still just as stupidly funny at nineteen,
            when we'd yell across a bonfire

Don't bogart that joint Goddamnit
      Nathaniel, Haven't I told you
            to pass the bong when you're through?

which is still funny to me even now—
      even though I look back and see,
            as I could not have seen then,

that Reverend Barker only stooped that way
      because he was dying,
            because cancer was eating his liver,

and because with each day
      it became both more urgent
        and more unlikely

that he would ever manage to say
      whatever it was he meant
            when he'd sit at the kitchen table,

or grip the black phone,
      or stand in the darkened driveway
            after we'd all gone home,

staring at the ground and saying nothing
      to his sweet, beloved boy
         but *Goddamnit*

Nathaniel, listen to me.
      Listen Goddamnit.
         Goddamnit Nathaniel, now listen.

My Lovely Assistant

After the episode of *That's Incredible!*
in which a whole family of Armenians
in sequined shirts ate fire
and spewed blue, burning plumes, my brother
tied a cottonball to a bent coathanger
and dipped the end in gasoline.

What made us who we are,
one crazy, fearless—one always afraid?
I stood by the ping-pong table
in our mother's only sparkly dress,
playing the role of *Patricia, Lovely Assistant*

because he was bigger than me,
and a master of the headlock,
and threatened, with his breath of snot
and bubble gum and cigarettes,
a vicious wedgy if I didn't.

So I handed him the silver Zippo,
not knowing what future waited for my brother,
still thinking I could save him
who hated being saved—

who took my dare one night to lie
on the yellow stripe of Brown's Bridge Road
and stayed there talking to himself,
pointing to a satellite adrift among the stars,
while I begged him to get up.

Who sat in an upstairs bedroom
giggling at the click of our father's .38.
Who loved the sting of the torch
sizzling his spit-glazed tongue.

So I kept one eye on the door, knowing
from experience how it would end,
how all things turned finally to anger

in that house, where he leaned back, shark-eyed,
and took a swig from the red gas can,
the spitting image of our father in a rage.
He stood between me and that pain.
Knowingly, he raised the magic wand up to his lips.
I sit and wonder what it means—
my brother's sweet face
bursting into flames.

Blue Ridge Bestiary

1. Vulture

Business never slows for the air's ubiquitous
morticians, their spiraling so effortless

we might admit its beauty if we didn't know
how eagerly, in those ridiculous black boas,

they wait to begin the endless dissipation
we take as proof: we've been forsaken,

unable to believe our angels of deliverance
rise even to the murky heaven of catfish.

2. Catfish

Greedy face of the zoot-suited villain
in a movie, sharpening his dagger-thin

moustache: sonsabitches I'd wish against
each time the bobber ducked and danced—

who swallowed all my best lures whole
and hissed, as with the crusted needle-nose

I ripped the hook and the hooked heart out
of a thousand, gasping cotton mouths.

3. Cottonmouth

The cure for life, said Socrates, is dying.
The cure for snakebite: slice your skin,

suck poison, then the guidebook says breathe
easily as the viper glides through brittle leaves.

A pit in its face can see your thudding heart.
Its flicked tongue tastes you sweating in the dark.

And even the severed head strikes with venom,
as if death's never dead, just playing possum.

4. Possum

Of all the corpses, none's more easily forgotten
than those bellies strewn beside the road. Rotten

entrails flaking into the treads of tires,
dark shapes hunkered on the lowest wires

as the whole scene flares in that brief brightness
through which we hurtle past each oracle, oblivious

of what it means to see them suffer
and rise from ashes on the wings of vultures.

David Scott Pointer

Film Time Flash to the Future

The way Mekong Delta blues
whiskey ignites the projector

The way the sniper knows
the nape of her unslit neck

The way water scorpions
scram w/o official direction

The way a hometown kid wears
a desert death box home

                unfilmed

Stephen Roger Powers

The Great Chicago Earthquake of 2002

The ghost of Mrs. O'Leary's cow spared the House of Blues
the night Dolly Parton teetered into that toddlin' town
in her pointed-toe mules with mile-high heels. She sang & picked
stripped-down bluegrass for gay standing-room-only
packed-to-overflowing city slickers. One flame too close
to her wig when she bent down to grab some roses
and the whole place could have gone up in explosions
gamboling from beer breath to beer breath,
cologne boa to cologne boa.
It was as far as you could get from the back porch
on Locust Ridge in Tennessee, where stamping feet
rumbled a hundred miles through ancient shale
and blue smoke all the way from the Mountain Opry
to her old autoharp and wooden chair rocking over the valley.
I was there in the stormy, husky, brawling freight handler
of the nation when it happened, when she plucked a stray
platinum hair dangling over her eye. The music slowed down
and high notes lowered to bass while it floated to her feet.
When it hit the floor of the stage she kept right on sailing
through "After the Goldrush," same speed as before.
Seismologists were puzzled the world over when
the corncob towers of Marina City swayed so much
they touched their tops. Long after the aftershock music
ended, and she was back in her custom purple Prevost
heading south, it was determined Dearborn was the unheard-of
epicenter. A shuffling janitor with a wide broom swept
that single hair into a dust bin.

Wyatt Prunty

Fields

Furrowed as the heaviest brow yet plain
As our forgetfulness, they are unmoved
By change, the way all origins lie stilled
By what they start. Long genealogies
Of fields rest in courthouse records
But lack what came before, generations
Nameless and permanent as need.

Rain, and the broadest reaches go under;
Drought, and they are dust. But always these remain.
To die down to stubble, to disappear,
Then rise from dark into the leaf-long change
Of new life—this carries more than reason
Gathers in its mirrors, as being fertile
After freezing cold or swallowing flood
Bears more than powers know to plant.

The Combine

rolled with the grace of a box
swallowing a path across the field,
dragging its skyline overhead,
till in the distance it became the fix

by which the day circled and stayed.
The cutting bars and feeder clanked,
filling the drum, as the whole thing lurched
with every turn, then repeated its way,

working the August air in which it ground
back and forth, stately and spare,
steadily going and going nowhere
but constantly around.

The chute exhaled, truck followed slowly,
as work meant cutting through one place
while running parallel in trace
for the yellowing wheat funneling lightly,

so the grain dust blazed as the low sun burned
and the hardwoods stood in silhouette,
bordering moment to moment
where the field waited and the combine turned.

Late Walks

Health was a brutally exclusive neighbor
With windows overlooking one-way streets
Where visits were brisk turns about sole topics
That either improved or did not, and where hope
Collected like some prospect of mass mailings,
Or the gloved applause of pigeons lifting.

Before she was sick, she said, she didn't know
What health *was* anyway, a free mortgage?
Carrying now what had grown too heavy,
I listened to her list of losses,
Diminishment-sharpened, as sun-astringent
As the clearing where she drank air, praised light.

Chelsea Rathburn

A Raft of Grief

"The raft that means 'a great number' is not related at all to the raft that carries people or their possessions in the water. The two words are homonyms. . ."
—Morris Dictionary of Word and Phrase Origins

If only there *were* a boat,
low and long and loaded
with all we'd brought or built:
the fatal inattentions,
anxieties and tics
that time had sanctified,
our good and bad intentions,
rages, lapses, and aches.
If only it were that easy,
to stand only ankle-
deep in the sullied water
hoisting our shared cargo,
sinking no further beneath
its weight. If only the boat
did not need a rower;
we'd push it off together
then wade to opposite banks
absolved at last, forever,
buoyant, watching it go.

The Talker

The details of his story aren't the point,
nor is the listener, who looked as bored
as we, two accidental eavesdroppers
in a London restaurant. The point is, well,
his point, which after ten long minutes
he came to abruptly, and with a flourish,
saying slowly and in perfect seriousness,
"All we are is dust in the wind. *All*
we are. Is dust. In the wind." I think
we bit our fingers to keep from laughing,
I know we mocked him through Paris, Barcelona,
Rome, and even years later, when one
of us became a little too serious,
the other would turn and quote his quote again,
jabbing the air as he had jabbed the air.
I picture him still sitting in some café,
proclaiming we were always born to run
or urging wayward sons to carry on
the way we tried to carry on, the couple
at the next table who couldn't help but listen,
with so little of our own to talk about.

Fire Ants

Jacksonville, 1983

Squatting in the coppery mud of the drainage ditch
behind my cousin's house, we searched for fish,
saw none. We found a speckled frog instead,
un-spooling a long, gelatinous thread
of black eggs in the water. Then fire ants—
my feet a blaze of pain, a fumbling dance,
and fact and memory begin to stutter.
What happened next? What curses did I utter?
And how did I ever get back over the fence?
I remember having a kind of reverence
for the whole affair: the pity I got, each bite
growing large and lustrous as a pearl, my tight
and swollen toes. I must have liked the pain.
What else would make me prod again, again?
A whole week hobbling barefoot on the lawn,
and still I missed the welts when they were gone.

219

Janisse Ray

Secret

I know where
the ribbon snake
lives—
under the maple
by the barn.
One day when I
was there
a dead leaf
crackled like fire
and I saw her,
slip of green
I followed
around the waist
of the tree,
through already
dying grass.
When she turned
to face me, eyes
burning, she
studied me.
I—wanting
to feel her softness,
her certainty, the stove
of her tiny heart—
touched one finger,
only one,
upon her perfect tail.
At that moment
the tree opened
and she wound
inside, her
passageway
dark and narrow.
Long before
I turned away,
no doubt,
she lay
on her mat of earth
at the bottom
of the maple,
among the roots,
strip
of brilliant
kindling.

Okefenokee Swamp

In this sweetwater wash, copper shafts of snakes
develop among cypress. Boles upstretch

to green bodices, the wrinkled circles of knees.
Thigh-like buttresses settle a trembling earth.

If it weren't for cypress the dark
water would dive forever.

Prothonatary warblers like small suns orbit
sweet bay magnolia with its white-threaded leaves

and the shed tongues of loblolly bay. Obsidian
channels penetrate the titi, shackled to the swamp's

emerald heart. Turtles are fluent in the act
of immersion. The sawgrass prairie is crisscrossed

with wakes. At its edge a great egret, stark
white and spindly, a black-stemmed flower,

curls into the landscape, wings outspread.
I close my eyes into its image, etched on the plates

of my lids, corrosion of landscape centuries old.
I am not afraid to die.

Land of Milk and Honey

An Homage

1. *milk*

the moon a pond of magnolia
petals. porcelain moonflowers
twining bleached bones
of deer. china saucers scraping
the whitewashed cupboard.
enamel pan. white-hot water singing
against the lacy skull of milch cow.
milkweed fluff tugged from its pod
by seven white horses of wind. breasts
beneath cotton gowns of ibis-winged
women. panting of the women.
cirrus throats of sparrows.
panther claw scratching
at a parchment window. moth papers.
hairs of my grandmother
cupping white eggs of doves.
powdery ashes of white oak, sifted
through the moon's cheesecloth.
fog of the morning of every
twig's birth and winter child's
breath tatting tiny flowers.
dew on gardenias like buttermilk.
meringue on a frothy creek.
tablecloth clattering its teeth.
the evening star hissing through
faded arms of white sycamore.

2. *honey*

slant of October sun on tupelo
hives. saddlebags of worker bees
spilling gunpowder to Sunday.
drone of barred owls.
catacombs of fertile eggs
from rusty chickens. iron bolts.
wagon tongues groaning
with the weight of coming night.
feathers of crowing cocks.
tannic Ten Mile Creek pouring

toward the golden river, morning
of the river. humps of cypress.
poplar hand-hewn into table,
axe-handle and bowl. sumac.
the hawk's red tail dripping
gallberry. wildflower fire
inside a brick chimney above
a thousand chipping sparrows.
thunder-showers of longleaf burrs,
early fall on red clay.
rainwater funneling toward
the branch, past stone crockery
filled with brown eggs.
outside the window, dun fields
of clover, millet, sorghum.
warm bread and an open jar.

Billy Reynolds

The Unfledged Ducks in the Abandoned Clarifier

The day is early enough that you can stand at the guard rail
and let the light hit you square in the face, let it bronze you
with its medallions that come and go as they wish.
You can stare down at those two vacuous holes
dried up for good, not even a tear in them,
like two perfectly round swimming pools so close they touch.
The water plant is rank with sulfur and god knows what else,
though everywhere I look are birds: on the road, a killdeer
stutter-steps, barn swallows cruise so low their wings brush the grass,
and Canada geese, near the creek's edge, nest in pampas grass,
and these right here, ten feet below us, dying to fly up and out.

The idea of the water plant is process: first the water
must pass through the screen so the solids are removed,
condoms, sticks, tampons, sand and grit, you name it,
though something always gets through, as it should,
apple and tomato seeds, lucky penny, everlasting pinecone.

But these can't rise, not yet. They stand in the shade
of the half-bridge scraper that once pushed the sludge
toward the bottom. Then they are all energy, so alive
they look forgotten, the trough they run in too much
like a bobsled track with sharp turns and steep banks,
until you think of the stale, two-week old bread in the break room.

John Fairbank, dead by now, or so I guess,
how we stood there and didn't move for hours. Late August,
and we wanted a pastoral—not these odd ducks shaming us
with their—I don't want to say it—cries for help.
I never saw you broken, never saw you race your heart out,
never saw you plow through that concrete trough that has no end,
never saw you bunched up among so many helpless others.

It is still summer, and you hang on the edge ready to drop down.
I'm on my belly snaked under the guardrail. By now I have my hands
on your wrist, waiting. It looks as if the entire sky is waiting.
If I could chase them, wave my hands in the air, but I can't.

If I could scoop them up one by one and make a nest
out of both hands, but I can't. If I could be a small caught bird. . .

One by one, you caught them all and lifted them up to me.
Unfledged, yellow, damp feathers—they too would fly.

Then my hand was in yours again, pulling you up,
behind us the retention ponds, and out beyond the wheat fields
the Red Cedar River where the potable water returns.
No words passed between us, even as you unlocked the gate
to the creek and the mother showed up, even as they followed her
through the gate and we heard them make their way down the steep bank,
scratching in such high grass, even as we watched them form
separate wakes, even through each head count you made,
each number mouthed without any sound, like a teacher asking
for a show of hands, each hand held higher and higher still.

Easter Garden

It had been weeks since we had spoken.
For once we didn't take ourselves miserably
home where my sister began a long descent
that simply ended on a jail floor and her burial
on my birthday in Starkville the narcissus in full bloom.
So I asked him and he said yeah
and came but came late and forgot the hoe.
That day it felt good to give up language,
the whole world reduced to transparent
gestures, to grunt, sigh, and pointing.
Sunday of dirt beneath my nails.
Sunday of blue on blue and discovery.
I hardly know what it meant to my brother,
but we fetched the wheelbarrow out of the truck
and hauled some dirt up from the creek.
We found an old loading pallet and broke
the handle off a broom and made a trellis, sort of.
Though I wasn't even going to be around
to watch the cucumber vines rise up each plank,
or sit down with him and eat our vegetables.
Though you could see we were getting tired of each other,
and already the first few hard stars were out,
and the yellow flowers that make me sigh for summer,
for I don't know what, were gone,
leaving only the blood-spit azalea blossoms,
leaving only my brother to say *ah lawd*—
half sigh, half why—half nothing in particular.

Jonathan Rice

Passover

When I heard you'd returned in the bay
of a C-130 as one in a row of other first ones

lost to indescribable flashes of light,
and that someone with your name tacked on

to the remains of her own waited with family
to receive you, I thought of your mother

the afternoon she took us up to Stone Mountain
to see the carving of horses and men—a fable

in granite—and how, because we'd forgotten
their names, she made us recite them verbatim—

yours and your father's among them—such
urgency in her, as though he'd just been

flown back from Da Nang—your birth
long months in the future—and everything

must be preserved. She was losing her mind
on the long train of Percodan, Oxycodone

and gin, too many pills and her breathing
laborious. The photo depicts her lean

to the left, exhaling to shutter that moment,
shepherded off from the rest of that day—

the haze of Atlanta hanging behind us—
before the night show and lasers, Ray Charles

ten stories high, singing Georgia on his mind.
You made me swear then, I remember exactly,

the moment Tina took over, before her record
skipped and caught in the squawking loudspeakers,

rolling and rolling—that we'd sign up
when we could, ship off, be gone—on the river,

she exalted at last to finish the song. And our
uncle was somewhere over Syria by then,

the pins of his rank and patches of a skull bared
by lightning and ship swarmed round with stars,

removed from his flightsuit, the Apache unpainted,
skimming nape-of-the-earth above goatherds

in the desert, his orders, he said, a clear series of steps
leading him back and down to the deck, to a bunk

and locker with the burden of his name inside
and two or three pictures, one of an orchard

where he'd walk again through the cool of an evening
to say to me: *Once or twice, I felt like the warrior they said I was.*

~

Let me say to you, Colin Lee, that it was Davis
and Jackson there beside your namesake,

and they were forty-two feet deep in granite
and four hundred feet above us twenty years ago.

And still, your father's name is as good as you left it.
Yesterday, in Richmond, I drove up one of the hills

of the city and waited for a sign out of the heat,
of how I should proceed—with no work, and our home

sold from under us—and thought of you, and knew
you were close, was sure you were there, and I had

nothing to say for myself. I left the car and walked out
under the bearing sun and stood at the edge of such

a small place—such a small city next to a bend in a river—
just as you stood at the bend of the Shatt-al-Arab,

staring out with Saddam's ninety-nine officers all standing
in bronze and pointing accusation—constant blame

heating and reheating in constant sun, too hot to lay a hand on
without burning—like the statues lining Monument Avenue,

Lee staring toward another burning capital, which burns
forever, I think, for him, remaining in rubble and smolder

for those who march in his name every year, in the sad
circles of heritage, of what is not anymore a remembrance

228

for any one of them. I stood at the fall line of the James
River, at the center place of the city's beginning, which was

the place of my beginning when I left home to not join up
and fly, or to avoid joining up and having to fake sick

to leave, like Stephen Mazel at Paris Island, after the trick
seniors played on him—*Yeah, let's go; we're all gonna sign on*—

and suddenly he was alone with sergeants, bootshine,
dogtags and a rifle. I stood over my city as you must've

stood over your assigned city in the desert, after the sudden
drop, the straight-down landing under threat

of ground fire, the C-130 disgorging live men and their gear,
and the only way out receding, even that last time,

inevitably. It might have been you, some miles from here,
saying by sign of the turkey vulture hovering in a hollow

updraft, or the silence itself. That evening I snatched a moth
from the air as it passed—the grease of its wings a silver

scaling drifting from my fingertips like salt or ash.
Then a memory of your only visit years ago, looking

at school, staying the weekend before heading back.
I wanted to show you the river and Belle Isle, the remains

of the prison camp there from the war, where men froze
and then more froze, and nothing's left but trenches,

a stone wall, a few signs that the city removes for months
at a time to clean of graffiti. And maybe I meant it as a reminder

or a warning to not sign yourself off overseas, ship out, get lost,
but you ignored me and walked out to the ledge by the water,

where the granite rose in an easy slope from the current
to submerge into woodline and the current of roots and all else

behind us, and pointed to a wide, crystalline streak in the stone
and said to me, *This is a fault. This is a fault of the earth.*

Folie à Deux

My father is a good man (or if your father is dead)
my father was a good man.
        –MMPI

In his story, it was the bloat of the body that silenced my father
to see a boy he did not know

but dove to find a meter beneath the waxed light
of lake water, and rose up with him on his shoulder

and laid him in the boat, and brought him home.

He was alone with us, years from there
and on the water too,

with us staring on as that part of his past passed forward.

~

I am bothered by an upset stomach several times a week.
At times I feel like swearing. I find it hard to keep my mind

on a task or job. My soul sometimes leaves my body.
The questions drown the sense out of themselves.

In relation to yes, to no, there's no telling. It is
eighty-two degrees. Yes, it's raining. Yes, I am here.

~

There is light slanting in from under the door. There is light
and no voice from the window. There is light from under

the door and no voice but hers. My wife
lies across the bed and waits for me but does not stare.

There's time for everything, I've been told.

~

In her story, I am trouble, and my mother knows it.
The doctor hastens to add, this one may be too much.

Your daughter is healthy.
Consent and everything else
are reserved for another day. During the drive home

my mother is alone and stopped at a train crossing
and cannot quit crying. There are no passengers

but coal and lumber, then slate. The train is miles long
and seeming to grow. Soon, I am four and have not yet spoken.

~

At times my thoughts have raced ahead faster than I could speak them.
Truth and time both have the same problem. During the past

few years I have been well most of the time. If a train had not left
Central at ten a.m. and another had not left Asheville

at eleven, and if these trains had not passed each other
at the crossing that my mother sat before

and had she not seen each rocking the wake of the other
in their tracks, would she have believed her body

to be like those tracks, and her children the lives intersecting
across them before her there, both as fast as they could

away from the other and both from her forever?

~

In the story of the boy in the water, the boy was put in the earth
before too long, and my father did not attend the service

or was not invited. For who would wish to meet the man
who confirmed the fear of a son drowning himself? And so

most of the memory ended there, but held him, and hollowed into us
for awhile, and we all sat silently. The sun set behind the house.

The patio grayed and grew dark with us, and soon we were blind
to each other, even as he rose for bed without speaking.

~

Once a week or oftener I become very excited. I believe my sins are
unpardonable. My wife moves about upstairs. I remain

below long enough to hear her feet leave the floor
to the bed. *I have very few fears compared to my friends.*

I almost never dream. Maybe another day, I know she's thinking,
it will take. It will. And then. *Sometimes my voice leaves me*

or changes, even though I have no cold. Already she has knitted
five sweaters in miniature, of varying colors, one with a hood.

They hang in the hall closet before the door. The dog turns
circles lying down and sighs. *At times I hear so well it bothers me.*

It is not winter, but cold comes so thoroughly into the room
that I shiver. *I enjoy gambling for small stakes.*

~

Should I kneel at the crib with my hands over our daughter's ears
so she can dream and wake and drift into dream again

without incessant murmurs all around? Will she wait to suffer seizure
tremor, or the barking of her name from an empty stairwell

and continue on unbaited? Will she say, *I would like to be a nurse,*
and then taking up the tones that I have given, *I have not lived*

the right kind of life? In the morning there is a shudder. Lord
do not let it be so. Father, do not let it be so. Have mercy.

Intercede for us. For I am foolish and troubled by my dreams.

The Least of Us

Lightning in the Eastern valley burned pampas grass
and pines across the barren—everything scattering

for cover, except a stubborn mare which burst apart
beneath a great oak in your neighbor's field. I was

young and leaving, had already left—your nape-hair
raised inside the living air through which we watched

the horse fall within a flash, and then to fill a backhoe
trench the morning after your uncle was shot—

an argument over the only working quarter gambler
in the county, in a gas station open too late.

The other man—too drunk to give a name when
asked who he thought he was—some Mexican,

an illegal with a chip there on his shoulder,
fucking call him juan or jesus, I don't care which,

your mother said. He'll be dead inside a year.
No it took ten—his name and story spit

in the far back end of the obits, there this last time
I was home and waiting for another one of us

to pass—my grandfather's lungs broke and filling—
drowning as the hospice nurse pushed against

the upraised portion of his breastbone. He was
telling her—Help me up. Help me get up.

Because the waters, they had risen, and no way
to get a breath. I remember your father—leaning

into the officer's shadow when they told him
his brother had walked fifteen, maybe twenty

feet after that first shot to the head—
how he was shrunken, bare-chested, mid-summer

brown, a stomach full of Miller and wanting to settle
with juan, said he'd take a pistol shoved down inside

his boot into the county lockup, after the police
had been dispatched elsewhere—the echo of a siren

barely present, whining past the highway and fruit
farms, the novelty of orchards near your neighbor's

barn and the wide field beside it, which was almost
always empty, his stable failing and then falling apart

after word spread that the sparse dirt patch—
that troubled ground beneath the oak char-split

down to its roots—was full of someone's horse.
Your father didn't even own a gun, didn't have a pair

of boots, could not approach someone for quarters,
for fucking quarters, hey man for lined up slots.

Ann Ritter

Toward Solstice

The light lies
in November. The undersides
of hickories reflect a yellow
which no longer exists,
come twilight.
That bright blush that leaves
wear comes from the shock
of cold. And

we are left with December days,
heavy, quiet air.
At dusk wood smoke
smells like olives.
Dark calls us home.
We draw into ourselves
for long sleeps,
toward a core
of light, waiting, still
as crocuses,
in black earth.

Etude

Caesar Franck's "The Doll's Lament"
is the only song my hands remember,
though I wear my watch face
inside my wrist as Miss Economy did,
and a ring very like hers. She promised
my fingers would grow to reach an octave-plus.
The lessons did not take, but much else did—
the smell of lemon polish on her black piano,
sight of honey-colored floors, and babble
she spoke to aging Greek parents
on the other side of a swinging door.
Once I went through their quiet house to the bath
where I rubbed the soap—so solemn an amber.

For seven years of Tuesdays, I arrived early,
waited for other lessons to be over, mine to start.
From the book case beside where I sat,
I devoured all of Pearl S. Buck and settled
on my favorite encyclopedia photo:
The Wildman of Borneo. I coveted
most of all a student's gift—a spicy, cloved orange
hanging from a red satin ribbon on the coat rack
in the corner. I came to love Chopin, because
his notes felt different to the touch, as if I sensed,
before being told, that he composed on the pianoforte.
Years later I cried when a Mozart concerto struck
not a piano key but the exact place in my heart
that missed the mother who insisted on those lessons.

Mulberry, Burnt Orange, Pistachio

The only time I remember
my grandmother running, she carried me
and a bucket. Its handle creaked.

The fire fit the words,
"conflagration" and "fully involved."
Before we saw it, we felt its draw,
heard its rush and hiss from deep
in the woods, down the dirt road.

The yard when we arrived was ringed
with buckets dangling from idle arms.
A rectangle of mulberry, burnt orange
and pistachio flames danced
among remaining two by fours,
had already eaten walls.

The crowd stood there wretched,
let the skeleton cave in on itself.
Grandmother held me tightly against her,
shocked to feel me straining
toward the bright, hot danger.

Liz Robbins

Studio

The couple in the rooms above me smoke. The smell
drifts down into their floor and through the cracks in my ceiling.
When I pass by them in the hall, they nod, *Hello, hello,* smile,
their arms bloomed with packages. He goes in daily
to an office. She travels to Paris with the airlines.
Once she came home with a sack overflowing with brie,
Gauloises, red wine. She smiled, shy, sideways. Down came
smoke, good silence, for days.

I lie in the dark. Dried roses, sage, scentless in a vase.
I inhale. The smell, the smell.

The man below me smokes also. The smell ascends
through his ceiling into the cracks in my floor. When I pass by,
he cries, *How are you?*, shows his teeth, leaves bowls of chicken
stew outside my door. He never seems to leave, has money
all his own, mysteriously. Once he painted his rooms a beautiful
whorehouse red. Blond men with long lashes come to his place
to stay the weekend. They play Moroccan music, sitars. Cook
with cumin and garlic. Stars shine beyond the windows, two
or three in bright clusters, and the occasional one, alone.

Dan Rosenberg

New Idioms

When the night is fully formed
but your pulse has the cadence of anticipation.
Loving and hating something simultaneously.
Cracking a pomegranate open
to find nothing but mist and hunger.
The pleasure of never having enough.
Homecoming to a place you've never been,
then remembering your daughter,
always afraid of new illnesses.
When you catch a spider in your fist,
take it out of your house and release it,
knowing your hand will feel dirty forever.
When you catch a spider in your fist
and hear the sound of laughter down the hall.
Your brain's sadness trumped by some
strange bird calling for his lover.
When your family surrounds you,
how grateful to be embarrassed by them.
The way Matryoshka dolls replace
psychology when the lights go out,
and how you can never find the smallest doll.
Sleeping behind a wall with no ears.
The secret lust for rainfall.
When you're left without a seam,
tiny, with no more empty spaces.
Your heavy club foot scatters your tracks.
The varied populations of the cusps.
Being born a dry orphan but finding
a tongue to call your own.
Speaking as if poorly of the dead.

Heaven

And when I asked for a round-trip ticket
she scoffed and scratched her wing.

And dandruff from that wing fell
to my elbow where another head
grew treacherously from the divine.

And I asked how many fish
must a man swim past until et cetera.

And the twelve beloved hamsters
of my youth were all present
in infinite plastic spheres
they moved with their paws.

And the honest men
interrogated themselves.
And they found the dirt worthy.
And they sold it.

And my back itches only enough
to satisfy the scratching of it.

And the great orange death breezed
right by us, looking lonely.

And one eye fell with a chopping motion.
And the thirsty world getting older.

And looking around for the Dodos they're
all right here.

And I touched a woman with wings
made of rain
and she moved my hand to where it fit.

And a slow mongoose curled
into her chest, rejecting the ravaged whatever,
and her new body grows, hardens.

And the gates are such worked threads.

And the gates pull one more dim curve.

Rosemary Rhodes Royston

On the Discovery of Aspirin

Could it have been a three-day headache—
the kind with the relentless throb and slam
of the sledgehammer, the sick roll of the eyes,
the ache in the base of the neck,
that drove someone into the woods
shrieking in two parts pain, one part delirium
just mad enough to rip off slender leaves
and shove them into his mouth, the bitter taste
bringing relief not long after,
       or was it the midwife, helpless
against the feverish flesh and moan
of the laboring woman, who ran into the dusk,
tearing bark from a tree while reciting a prayer
in some unknown language, later helping
the baby make its way into the world
as the mother's skin cooled and she wept
softly, like a willow moving in the breeze.

Jenny Sadre-Orafai

Foiled Season

Flood of leaves, little artifacts, just vulgar signs
of fall. It's a season that suffocates this smallest smack-
ing in my chest. I plant scarecrows in every corner.
They wear his cashmere sweaters, paint-tainted pants,
cowhide gloves better than him. These straw men
won't be off. They man their posts. He's not allowed
here since he stole this four roses mouth from other men,
since he brought poison to this once sturdy crop.

Angelle Scott

The Men Who Sit Under the Trees

Trees grow on the neutral ground:
their roots struggle up to the surface,
break up the grass,
form hills and valleys in the dirt,
crack the concrete curb.

Plastic chairs circle the trees:
the legs are uneven,
as some are propped on the roots
and some sink into the mud
created by stomping feet and scraping wheels.

Men sit in the plastic chairs:
their dirty, cracked fingers play
over the dirty, cracked plastic
as they smoke many packs of cigarettes
and drink many bottles of Thunderbird.

More men sit in wheelchairs:
dwindled legs dangle;
cut-off khakis flutter in the breeze;
colostomy bags rest warm and heavy;
wheels cut grooves into the ground.

Sweat rolls down the men's bodies:
drops slide down exposed Buddha bellies,
collect in swiftly darkening waistbands,
perch on the tops of lips,
fall into mouths sour from beer.

The men sit under the tree every day:
they call out to those *young gals*
who switch their bottoms as they walk;
they pick off caterpillars and flies;
they rub the stickiness out of their bloodshot eyes.

M.E. Silverman

The Mud Angel of Macon

ends on two lines from Pedro Salinas

In the barn, he removes
and folds his clipped wings,

a blue-gray from age
like the dye in elderly ladies' hair.

The long feathers brush
the scar on his left cheek,

and every morning, it itches
like a healing wound open to air.

He looks down from the loft,
rests a hand on one bale of hay,

thinks about chores and closes
the trunk, thick with dust and dirt,

then turns, his back bare
like ghost limbs.

Earth. Nothing more.
Let that be enough.

Separation Grows

like bindweed or rattlebox
across a field, covers the decent
between us: the seasonal burnings
where smoke and ash touch.
The harvest will rise without us,
or perhaps, despite us,
as the geography of orchards
gives in to the wild.

The geometry of barns equates a mathematics
we choose to forget, moments spent shaping
days devoted to dirt
until the passion for space and distance
develop into concerns of the now
and the next now,
until all the words for love curl away
like cast-off wire-wrap from brown boxes.

From inside the bay window,
I see the sun drop like a yolk
into the horizon's pan. I watch
a wasp tap its whole body,
tap against each pane,
where warmth and pollen
are a paradise away.

Why There Is No Fifth Season

i. *Leaves*

For Mother, the fifth season arrived—
a *Farmer's Almanac* of second chances.

Another house to fix,
another town to touch.

Several roses jut
while other petals swell

through the missing wattle board
from the fence he never fixes.

Neighbors notice the weeds
while no one sees

the sun-soaked lace
in the bottom of the shed

on top of a tulle veil
or hydrangeas she presses

into *Twenty Love Poems
and a Song of Despair*.

ii. *Working in Forsyth*

After my mother pots her last plant,
she kneels at the yard's edge
with her old trowel, two acres away
from the half-painted house,
two people removed
from Father in his office,
pretending to finish his doctoral work:
the Miltonic apple and the *felix culpa*.

I read Forster and Eliot.
One says *I quite expect to end
my life caring most for a place*.
The other types lines like
Houses live and die.

The phone line blurs gray
with shrikes or mockingbirds.

Three plastic butterflies
whirlygig in the alley
between a fence and shed.

I'm sitting cross-legged.
In my lap, a stuffed dog,
a small blanket, folded neat,
under a bag of travel toys
and a Shel Silverstein book.

Everything is off-centered
around two tickets for a one-way
viewliner roomette to St. Cloud,
already in the taut grip
of Mother's left hand.

James Malone Smith

Frequencies

Cows bawling.
Hear it every fall when we take the calves,
hear it into the nights, all week,
wake up to it. One daybreak years back
I stumbled out of bed
                      hearing a baby
but he was already six.
That night in his prayers, he asked God
make it stop.
And amen.

Everything here seems hard—
trying to keep things alive
long enough to kill them.
Half drunk on the porch in the dark, mainly drunk,
I might fiddle with this staticky radio all night, cursing at
that big ugly shrub by the mailbox
                            but that's no good.
No way to figure it.
Horses stabled until morning.
The woman and child washing dishes.
A man shaking his radio
switches it off.

But, now. *Listen.*
                  I'm listening now
in the cricket quiet.
                  It stopped.
Those cows near the fence.
Listen close,
           you can hear
the grass snapping.
                Plates clink,
and laughter from the kitchen.

The Boathouse

We turned back from the bay while light still hesitated.
You said, "Can't see how you lived
here all this time, and never fished, or swam, or sailed,"
but I found the poison-ivied path down
to the old stone boathouse with its rotten roof.
Watery light shimmered inside the arches
boats once glided through.
Among rafters the water-glimmer
blinked into blackness. From there boats had lowered.

We dodged ivy up to the shadowy road,
and I listened: the contentious
cats, the garage half-painted, dad's bad back,
how my brother makes you cry, his heartbreaking
tenor voice, four long tables of food at the reunion, which I missed,
everyone dancing. Hermit or wastrel,
alternating months, years, never in the sun, I heard myself
promise, *promise*. I watched us walk on into night, heard the hoist unreel,
then catch.

The Captive

I study your face like your chalkboard.
Some nights before you erase it, I look for clues
you may have scribbled by mistake, your footprints
foxlike backtrackings in the chalk dust.

Your grimace in sleep often frightens me,
and I will lean nearer, just as you murmur something,
smiling now, as if you've played another good trick—
hidden somewhere you could not be found.

To put you to bed, I at last have to brandish my belt.
And you always fall, heroically, asleep.
But as I ease out of the room, I keep watch
until I have closed the door between us.

Tonight as you fought dreaming, muscles
jumping, eyelids quivering, fists,
$\qquad\qquad\qquad\qquad$ a cricket piped up
chirping in your room.
$\qquad\qquad\qquad\qquad$ From every corner, chirps
ricocheted off your dome of sleep. I cursed, quietly,

grabbing in slow motion at books, Tonkas,
bears, everything almost, the air—
until I caught him. He held still and I held my breath.
He throbbed as I kept him in my cupped hands.

Then he sang out.
$\qquad\qquad\qquad\qquad$ He bumped against my palm,
singing out and bumping against the palm of my hand,
hopping mad.
$\qquad\qquad\qquad$ What else could I do? I let him go, let him sing,
and you slept.

Leon Stokesbury

The Day Kennedy Died

Suppose that on the day Kennedy died
you had a vision. But this was no inner movie
with a discernible plot or anything like it.
Not even very visual when you get down
to admitting what actually occurred.
About two-thirds of the way through 4th period
Senior Civics, fifteen minutes before
the longed-for lunchtime, suppose you stood up
for no good reason—no reason at all really—
and announced, as you never had before,
to the class in general and to yourself
as well, "Something. Something is happening.
I see. Something coming. I can see. I . . ."

And that was all. You stood there: blank.
The class roared. Even Phyllis Hoffpaur, girl
most worshipped by you from afar that year,
turned a vaguely pastel shade of red
and smiled, and Richard Head, your best friend,
Dick Head to the chosen few, pulled you down
to your desk whispering, "Jesus, man! Jesus
Christ!" Then you went numb. You did not know
for sure what had occurred. But less than one hour
later, when Stella (despised) Vandenburg, teacher
of twelfth grade English, came sashaying
into the auditorium, informing, left and right,
as many digesting members of the student body
as she could of what she had just heard,
several students began to glance at you,
remembering what you'd said. A few pointed,
whispering to their confederates, and on that
disturbing day they slinked away in the halls.
Even Dick Head did not know what to say.

In 5th period Advanced Math, Principal
Crawford played the radio over the intercom
and the school dropped deeper into history.

For the rest of that day, everyone slinked away—
except for the one moment Phyllis Hoffpaur
stared hard, the look on her face asking,
assuming you would know, "Will it be ok?"

And you did not know. No one knew.
Everyone staggered back to their houses
that evening aimless and lost, not knowing,
certainly sensing something had been
changed forever. *Silsbee High forever!*
That is our claim! Never, no never!
Will we lose our fame! you often sang.
But this was to be the class of 1964,
afraid of the future at last, who would select,
as the class song, Terry Stafford's *Suspicion.*
And this was November—even in Texas
the month of failings, month of sorrows—
from which there was no turning.
It would be a slow two-months slide until
the manic beginnings of the British Invasion,
three months before Clay's ascension to the throne,
but all you saw walking home that afternoon
were the gangs of gray leaves clotting the curbs
and culverts, the odors of winter forever
in the air: cold, damp, bleak, dead, dull:
dragging you toward the solstice like a tide.

Nemerov's "A Primer of the Daily Round" Held as a Mirror Up to Nature

A peels an apple, while B kneels to God . . .

What, for instance, do you suppose might prove to be
the significance if I were to dismiss class fifteen minutes
early tonight, and each of you, as you stride out
into the descending purple cloaks of dim and gloom,
each of you reaching your sundry parking lots
just a bit lighter, because of this slight but sudden
surprising slip of time, each of you igniting
your Probes, Explorers, Mirages, and Charades,
and tooling back into traffic beneath the Cimmerian dusk—
what, now, might the import prove to be,
as you stream toward your various destinations
surrounded by a completely different array of vehicles
than if I had set you free at the usual 7:30
instead of 7:15?
        And what consequence, do you suppose,
might be claimed, if the car in the lane next to you, odd car,
bad car, old car, Volkswagen of some kind, swerves rapidly
into your lane, creating a decidedly unpleasant union
and—in the same way a concrete bust of Elvis
placed upon a three-foot concrete pedestal
in your own backyard becomes the emerald ivy
that it's set among, and like the October umbra of oak
and pine that concrete bust of Elvis rests beneath
becomes that bust of Elvis in return—
your bumpers intertwine, osmotic becomings
 beneath the bleak, black sky?
        And as you stumble
enraged from your, say, cobalt blue Impala, you see
with such clarity the immediately beloved other—
trembling, stunned, numb—not at all
the jousting argumentative you had pre-conceived,
and as you stand there, lonely two, at the murky swirling center
of an empty ocean, exchanging State Farm insurance cards,
telephone numbers too, you hold the two cards
in your hand, side by side, thinking these insurance cards
are like these cars, conjunctive, these cars like the two
of you, or they could be, couldn't they, you think, and cast
a quick glimpse as she slides, but slowly, back
inside: Latin eyes and lashes, looking down, skin
shining, silk beneath her Volkswagen's interior lighting—
things can become analogous, can't they, just by being
placed in tandem, just by happening in a line.
        You

want only to forgive her, now, to let her know
she is already forgiven, more, to ask her to forgive you,
not for what you've done, but what you might do
someday, in some distant year, distant town, grit
in the bed, the incessantly noisy motel ice machine
across the hall—and for a second you are sure she would
if you might ask, if only you were not too yaller-
yaller-yaller-bellied to begin. Why, even art holds up
such random linkages, you almost say: *Hail in August,
Landscape with Summer Snow, Desert Rain*. But
the moment is gone, ephemeral, like little powdery flecks
of glaze falling off the doughnut of the world. *Young Man
with Thumb Up Butt*. And now she is smiling, thanking
you, apologizing again. O my contiguous, you think, O
my juxtaposed!

      She looks down once more, then drives off
pocked and pounded, but able, so it seems, to negotiate
her path amongst the massive, dark turbidity. And thus
it begins. A week goes by. Your nerve returns. Then
you do call and ask her to dinner. And a year goes by
before you marry, and then nine years go by, ten years total
from this very night and my releasing you soon enough
into the seemingly desultory caprice of evening, O
my adjacents, ten years before the blood and public pain
and lies and her living somewhere close to Albuquerque
last you heard. But still you can remember those long lashes
looking down: *Still Life with Red Pepper*: handing you
her State Farm insurance card, as if it were this very night,
tonight, which it is, the vision undiminished, pungent,
strong like that lingering zing left on the tongue
from consuming a more-than-acceptable Gorgonzola—
and then it is you recall this lecture, remember these
fifteen minutes, discern at last what consequence
might be claimed: nightshade, scimitar, guillotine,
future plans for gunfire being brought to bear.
          So,
go now, my tangentials, wind your weary ways
out amidst this mere shank of the gloaming,
like children in an autumn garden, orphans in a storm,
night dew dripping off the wilting topiary—
some toward domiciles, some to perform your brazen
stand-ups and sit-downs in the gin joints of your choosing—
little molten ingots marching as to war, two by two,
considering, perhaps, the essential nature of side meat
to the American breakfast. Green eggs and ham.
The comic genius of Curly Howard. *Nude at the Window.
Study in Burnt Sienna. The Menaced Assassin.
The Persistence of Memory. Twilight's Last Gleam.*

Watching My Mother Take Her Last Breath

People ground down by what the doctors call
"acute COPD" have not much but a vacuum
left inside when the ache of that last onset
invades the hospice air. But even though
that's so, and even though there came a time
when what she wanted most was just to sail
away, the body holds some tenets of its own.
There, at the end, I saw my mother's mouth
become a perfect round, a ring, a dark hole
clearly larger than it ever seemed before—
and it strove, I thought, through the scrim
of morphine, to draw into that dim chasm
everything it could. O, let the earth be
shoveled in, it seemed to say. O, let now be
consumed into this disk of dark, this gape,
the air and every small or massive entity—
all this lonely, frightened, wanting, weary,
sad and hurting woman has throughout
her little and long life never known. And then,
the heaving ceased. And the great shroud of the sea
rolled on as it rolled five thousand years ago.

Alice Teeter

Stones

She wanted to know   she asked
not long before she died   I answered
fingers over my mouth   my voice
muffled

Forgiveness is a slow slow turn
of many rocks or the same one rolled
again and again   a painstaking look
at the veins of quartz
a test of surface with tongue
see what shines   the dirt and bits
of leaves brought in   the tang of
swallowed grit   between the teeth
the crunch   brittle in the ears

It takes a lot of wary cleaning
the watchful piling up of many stones
to understand all of what you forgive
and whom

Kathleen Thompson

Lament

–for Ivodean

If we had simply walked the sands
of Seacrest an hour earlier this morning

before the emerald water was pinked
and skirted with foamy frilly-edged waves;

if the sea turtle had swum that great seaway
more slowly, if the undertow had been stronger,

tugging her away from her destined stop
just below the line of peat and sea oats;

if her lumbering, laboring steps through sand
had been less straight, less determined;

then we might have seen her begin the dig,
might have observed the high drama of that act,

its flawless timing, her eyes locked ahead
as the first contraction hit, an egg dropped out

until one hundred or so were safely covered
to foil hungry seagulls and sand pipers

crazed at the notion of eggs, eggs,
eggshells under such staggering weight,

a paradox we might have witnessed up close,
forgetting our complex pains, watching hers.

Natasha Trethewey

Elegy

—for my father

I think by now the river must be thick
        with salmon. Late August, I imagine it

as it was that morning: drizzle needling
        the surface, mist at the banks like a net

settling around us—everything damp
        and shining. That morning, awkward

and heavy in our hip waders, we stalked
        into the current and found our places—

you upstream a few yards, and out
        far deeper. You must remember how

the river seeped in over your boots
        and you grew heavier with that defeat.

All day I kept turning to watch you, how
        first you mimed our guide's casting

then cast your invisible line, slicing the sky
        between us; and later, rod in hand, how

you tried—again and again—to find
        that perfect arc, flight of an insect

skimming the river's surface. Perhaps
        you recall I cast my line and reeled in

two small trout we could not keep.
        Because I had to release them, I confess,

I thought about the past—working
        the hooks loose, the fish writhing

in my hands, each one slipping away
        before I could let go. I can tell you now

that I tried to take it all in, record it
        for an elegy I'd write—one day—

when the time came. Your daughter,
        I was that ruthless. What does it matter

if I tell you I *learned* to be? You kept casting
        your line, and when it did not come back

empty, it was tangled with mine. Some nights,
        dreaming, I step again into the small boat

that carried us out and watch the bank receding—
        my back to where I know we are headed.

On Captivity

Being all Stripped as Naked as We were Born, and endeavoring to
hide our Nakedness, these Cannaballs took [our] Books, and tearing
out the Leaves would give each of us a Leaf to cover us. . .
—Jonathan Dickinson, 1699

At the hands now
          of their captors, those
                    they've named *savages*,
          do they say the word itself
savagely—hissing

that first letter,
          the serpent's image
                    releasing
          thought into speech?
For them now

everything is flesh
          as if their thoughts, made
                    suddenly corporeal,
          reveal even more
their nakedness—

the shame of it:
          their bodies rendered
                    plain as the natives'—
          homely and pale,
their ordinary sex,

the secret illicit hairs
          that do not (cannot)
                    cover enough.
          Naked as newborns,
this is how they are brought

to knowledge. Adam and Eve
          in the New world,
                    they have only the Bible
          to cover them. Think of it:
a woman holding before her

the torn leaves of *Genesis*,
          and a man covering himself
                    with the Good Book's
          frontispiece—his own name
inscribed on the page.

Knowledge

—after a chalk drawing by J. H. Hasselhorst, 1864

Whoever she was, she comes to us like this:
    lips parted, long hair spilling from the table

like water from a pitcher, nipples drawn out
    for inspection. Perhaps to foreshadow

the object she'll become: a skeleton on a pedestal,
    a row of skulls on a shelf. To make a study

of the ideal female body, four men gather around her.
    She is young and beautiful and drowned—

a Venus de' Medici, risen from the sea, sleeping.
    As if we could mistake this work for sacrilege,

the artist entombs her body in a pyramid
    of light, a temple of science over which

the anatomist presides. In the service of beauty—
    to know it—he lifts a flap of skin

beneath her breast as one might draw back a sheet.
    We will not see his step-by-step parsing,

a translation: *Mary* or *Katherine* or *Elizabeth*
    to *corpus, areola, vulva.* In his hands

instruments of the empirical—scalpel, pincers—
    cold as the room must be cold: all the men

in coats, trimmed in velvet or fur—soft as the down
    of her pubis. Now, one man is smoking, another

tilts his head to get a better look. Yet another,
    at the head of the table, peers down as if

enthralled, his fist on a stack of books.
    In the drawing this is only the first cut,

a delicate wounding: and yet how easily
    the anatomist's blade opens a place in me,

like a curtain drawn upon a room in which
each learned man is my father

and I hear, again, his words—*I study
my crossbreed child*—a misnomer,

the language of zoology, natural philosophy.
In this scene, he is the preoccupied man—

an artist, collector of experience; the skeptic angling
his head, his thoughts tilting toward

what I cannot know; the marshaller of knowledge,
knuckling down a stack of books; even

the dissector—his scalpel in hand like a pen
poised above me, aimed straight for my heart.

Rachel Trousdale

Lost in the Woods

As I wander into you I drop, every fourth step,
a white pebble, round and clean
as a skull, in the closing avenue of trees.
There's something ahead: a light? a fire?
the phosphorescent breathing of the swamp?
There's bread in my pocket. I'll find out.
But the woods are full of warblers, little
pretty brown flickering things.
Lacking their own teeth, they require
something definitive with which to grind
their food. They flick, they stoop.
Slowly the path behind me disappears.

Memye Curtis Tucker

Ghosts

The ghosts of my grandmothers
will not be trifled with
or teased into speech—
they have already spoken. Now they watch.

Wax in the proper places,
smiles, sacrifice, no salt on silver,
children warned of the undertow,
a glass of milk for the stranger at the door,
as little lying as possible, as little truth—

they want such things remembered
and no jot or tittle more—
no sniveling *early to bed, waste not*—
they are awake all night,
they wasted nothing
and still want everything.

I try to satisfy them.
But I spill the milk, grow tired,
tell strangers
what I suspect of the truth.

Yet I speak with their voices,
lie under their quilts,
bear their hand-me-down names:

no man owns us,
but we own each other:
our lives are one long life,

milk, child, myth—
on good days
bequeathed like family silver.

I polish the spoons,
holding them up to the dark.

Radishes

Not that I'd have made a gardener.
But my grandfather couldn't bear to give up
even one sunny row he had carved.
Only this garden was left
of his childhood's thousand-acre farm,
the part-acre where he ladled

black dirt and chicken droppings,
turning them over in red clay,
where each spring he helped me climb
to the back of the hired plow mule
for a bony ride down the driveway.

Everything had come down to borders
of chickenwire and fenceposts.
He couldn't shrink it more for a careless girl
who'd forget to water and weed, who'd
had life on a silver platter.

So he gave me the shade
of the wide-leafed fig tree,
and the radishes I harvested
were long, thin specters.

As summer came on, his dark furrows
leafed into rows of lettuce, mint,
butterbeans, corn, okra, two paths
of flowers his wife would exchange for prizes.
The figs grew heavy, sweet, warm.

Perhaps he meant to save me from the need
that every day hurried him home
from his office to swap a coat and vest
for overalls, a palm-smooth hoe.

And afterwards, to sit in the sun
with a pipe, his mended straight chair
leaning back against the garage,
the brim of his felt hat shading
eyes the color of mine.

Though I knew it was not my fault,
it was the spot that had failed,
one futile crop would be enough
for a lifetime.

Dusk in College Park

Sit with me on the cold front steps
to wait for the air raid warden
who comes in the dark to protect us.
I tell you with some pride—
he is my grandfather,
who died thirty years ago,
a man of unalloyed constancy.
This afternoon, something nuclear
fell into the Indian Ocean.
Nothing fell on Rugby Avenue
in the soft dusk
at the one door in the world
that never changes,
where my grandfather,
flashlight muffled,
invisible to the enemy,
walks his watch by moonlight.

Mimi Vaquer

Ode to a Fence

Your face has failed you, the skin falling in white chips
on a plumbago bed, angular snowflakes
refusing to melt or sink softly in the dirt.

Pinwheels of brown peek through the stippling
of paint and link your lineage to the pine tree infantry
that stands in stoic formation just miles from your post.

You stand on guard in shabby uniform, still hiding
the sight of passerby eyes from the small square of patio
at the heel of a great lady,

six-storied shy, hiding her graces in the shade of a noble oak,
some sort of cousin I'm sure, the upper arborial class
that bows "adieu" in the shadows of the sliding sun.

Kevin Vaughn

Home Opener

Athens, Georgia

By kickoff, Seventh Day Adventist pews are cold.
& tomorrow, bleary-eyed Baptists stomp
& sing & praise their victorious
Bulldogs, or curse their loss. Catholic

co-eds confess to their post-game nights
& are relieved not of sin, but pledge anew
into the Sisters of Saturday: daughters & mothers,
French manicures, hair bleached to the roots,

their black & red dresses cut high
& low. Like eunuch priests in red polo shirts,
polite, neatly pressed men who look fit to settled
hobbies—stamps, sudoku, Kinky Friedman

novels—debate out-of-towners
until they turn rageful pink
& upon the Bulldog's loss weep
into the skirts of their wives. Black

men hold cardboard signs & form a corona
of disinterested scalpers throughout the city.
By law, they maintain a distance
from the stadium. Monday's police blotter

details the student tackled naked
with an empty Jack Daniels bottle
& stabbing of an away team booster. *The Red
& Black*—the student rag—feigns shame

if the Bulldogs win. Saturday is Athens clearly—
tents, Styrofoam, widescreen TVs
& one-hundred tons of rubbish
ankle deep over the campus green.

There are no street names during this season
where the stadiums' chant echoes through weekdays
& trees' passage from green to gold.
You enter this queer pastoral, or turn another way.

New Way Cleaners

Athens, Georgia

From bumper stickers to counter talkers
  Boosting the conservative candidate,
    My dry cleaners are gray siblings:
A thin-haired bachelor & sister with a smile
Straight as the racks stretching into the dark.

Liberal, but teaching the art of thinking
  In a red state's only blue town,
    With dry cleaners & freshmen,
I dodge politics. Desperate as the entire
Country for elevated air, I ask the sister

About the best mountains. They cross
  The north. Every pick up afterwards
    I shutter, do not confess my fear of O'Connor's
Caution: Sun ought not set on a Negro
In the north Georgia mountains.

Change arrives—late & destitute,
  A seven decade business ends—
    On the front page of the *Banner-
Herald*. I tell the sister I will miss her smile
& blame not seeing the mountains

On poverty & lack of a car.
  They have no heirs who want
    To inherit both a laundry & Georgia heat.
And, she says, smoothing my shirts.
You want to do things while you still have time.

268

Metamorphosis

Sapelo Island, Georgia

I. *Waxing Gibbous*

This is not the coast of boyhood—
knotted sinews of sand,
tidal pools where waves deposit
vestigial Pangea, ash of our continued drift.

I am no longer a boy:
I notice my skin looser.
My smile disarms the few island women, but
the gray in my beard hangs like Spanish moss
& spectacles mask my crows' feet

& those creases are a helpless hurt.
Mornings, I plunge my hands into the pools.
Curious fishes inspect, dart away while
I smear my arms & chest & face with sand,
wait for the sun to fix the sediment.
Surely the sea will corrode my age;

everything fails in the salt air.
Every bolt, nail & fitting
of the wooden pavilion has rusted
through. Does the foundering strength
of a thousand galvanized dies
hold aloft the pavilion

or is the battery of storms & salt air a test
of faith that our lives will not leave us?
The rite of spilling sand is infinite, such is vanity
if I believe that with the sand, my life departs me.

II. *Waning Crescent*

Sapelo passed backwards
from a founder of the jet age
to a tobacco baron when Howard E. Coffin sold
the island R.J. Reynolds who promised the natives
electricity, indoor plumbing, parallel roads
& a bullet if they farmed or stepped
one foot beyond their unyielded plots.

Hog Hammock is four-hundred-thirty-four
contiguous acres for descendants of slaves
whose hands wristed indigo
& wrote on a table at the pavilion
for intrepid visitors to read:

I am a Salt Water Geechee.
I live on Sapelo, was born here and hope
to die here. This is as close to heaven
as you will get on Earth

2009, the year of our lord.
On Sundays, the ferry delivers mainland survivors
who pass the sweltering day
entire in their bright church ensembles.

I envy how they know their home.

III. *Full*

I arrived on this beach wan & agnostic,
now bronzed, filled—
from the pavilion
I watch the moon hover, labor, break
finally through the crimson haze
into a silver nugget
flushed by the clashes of heat—
the terrible, thunderless lightning.

Stabs of viridescence reveal
ghost crabs peering out
their burrows. Baby alligators
invisible, eager to poach the nests of sea

turtles. I sweep my red lamp—
over the boomerang-flippered tracks
toward the waves. If my need to see involved
no shame, no peril of sudden claws & teeth,
I would step nude into the drink.

IV. *2nd Quarter*

Nights, sitting on the pavilion
I stare out & wonder who I am
in the total absence of light.

I cannot negotiate with the many
who lamented the moon's cratered indifference
& waves' dark flesh
& scientists who take their daily measurements,
but do not love the salt marsh as I do—

nights when pitch & alligator eyes swallow your headlights,
the ubiquitous song of toads & the sudden huff of the bull
who haunts the crumbling autobahn in the wee hours.

V. *New*

As Earth enters Perseids, my hesitance dissolves.
Weeks have passed & my skin glows,
renewed by nightly floats in the bioluminescent loam.

The packed & lonesome sand no longer frightens me.
The sea could seize all but my clothes
& spectacles at the bottom step of the pavilion
during my unperturbed focus upwards
on the streaking stars, a blazing Jupiter. I recede
with the retreating tide until the lights of trawlers
idling in the distance glide lazily towards shore
warning me back like reluctant Morningstars.

On my final night with Sapelo, the tide is low,
the waves break too far from me
& clouds obscure in total my view
of the crescent moon and stars.

We part now as kin, hostile with farewell.

Dan Veach

Ancient of Nights

A windless night.
in the porch light
the bushes rustle and sway
without the least hint of a breeze.

We freeze—
Whatever it is, it's
not human.
Then,

a nose
the barest snout
appears in the light
a head, an eye

calm and completely unconcerned
looks out. A foot
steps high and carefully out of the weeds.
The thick white fur, the naked tail—

A possum!
Then another
smaller, darker,
brindled like a cat.

We watched them,
quiet, breath held,
in suspense
they moved

to the selfsame step
and dance,
tail to nose and nose to tail,
archaic, grave, intent

wild beyond beauty or ugliness, they went
down the pine needle path

slowly and carefully, swaying,
stepping high,

wholly unperturbed
by the last million years,
by human beings like us
and all we meant.

It was an eerie, wonderful event,
just as our ancestors must have felt
watching Neanderthal Man walk by—
knowing that if we should ever fail

out there on the night's dark tree
another branch of the mammal family
still waits to tell
its strangely different tale.

William Walsh

My Grandfather's Christmas Tree

My father and I stopped by my grandfather's house
for a snowball fight and some chicken
noodle soup. I helped my grandfather
carefully place the ornaments in tiny boxes
and wound the lights around my arm,
placing everything in a larger box,
then into the attic. My grandmother
was at the mall returning her new vacuum
when my grandfather shoved the Christmas tree
straight up the fireplace, just jammed it up there
with my father's help because as he said, "By God,
Christmas ended at midnight!" He struck the match.
Flames shot out the chimney, twenty feet
into the air. I knew we were in trouble.
After the fire department put out the fire,
I remember my grandmother's face looking out
from behind the windshield as her red Mercury
slow-coasted into the driveway, my father's hands
tightening on my shoulders.

Betsy Weir

For a Child Leaving Home

Gone the thunder of music, furious
dance, horror movies—gory to me

hilarious, you said—books in unsteady
piles throughout the house,

flip flops scattered at random
on which your dog rested her head

in hopes you'd take her with you.
Gone, too, the phone chatter,

algebraic equations,
notes for an essay due

the next day—punctuated with spasms
of laughter. Gone the lightness of air

these days, your way of explaining
any dilemma with rational delicacy.

I watched you grow steadily from
that tiny being into a young woman

who managed a full month in Europe
without my presence. I recall that time you

portrayed a brazen flirt in my clothes
at your school's play. That's when

you saw me almost fall out of my chair
from laughter and yes, pride, too.

Now tonight I can sleep in your bed,
curl up in the lingering scent

of your presence,
the curve of your absence.

Kelly Whiddon

Thumbing for a Hitch

I was made somewhere
along a road, one with thistles
in ditches and rattlers
and five boys,
of hitches hauling nuts
and whistles at bitches,
hauling cotton and soy
and boys
who would not listen
and, fervid and twisted
and smelling
of sweat, and listless, I shifted
and shoved my brother
and saw my mother in the cab,
who watched with gravid
face and eyes misty,
who turned away from
the livid, the lively,
the lathered smack
that sent me into
August air, that sucked
my wind, that slapped
to the bare and raw
and crusted rough
of road,
the cuff and whack
that forged us,
the wallop and cut
of me and it, the grit, the spit.
Is he dead, is he dead, is he dead?
they said, the white haired
couple on a porch
in the scorch of hot sun
watching me eat and hug
road and bug.
And so
the truck never came back
and the lack it gave, the grave
of ditch, the layers of lick,
the rhetoric
of road and load and mode
of trick and lesson played,
was where, and how, and when
I was made.

Dirty Glass

When my brother shot himself,
there were no clean dishes.
Plates stood stacked, buried
in breakfast. That afternoon, I pulled a dirty
glass from the sink, began washing
it with bathroom soap till my brother stormed
in, fought with father, and trudged
to the front bedroom where walls
were white, and the window
framed the dirt road leading to anywhere.

Mother was dead,
and we slept on gritty sheets or bare
mattresses, buttons brandishing backs,
clothes hung back up before washing,
and we would drink from Mason jars,
look through hazy glass windows at fields
layered in dust, and want to be
beyond them.

A brown ring clung
to the glass, residue of sweet tea
my father drank, crystals of his extra
sugar settling around the rim,
and a bubble formed in the middle,
captured the light in the kitchen window,
creating an opalescent shimmer,
pink and brown, on the waxy
surface.

The house trembled
just enough to shake the tea bubble, pop
it. I dropped
the glass, breaking it into pieces still
soaked in brown bubbles,
              fragments where my father's fingers
              left a fuzzy print.

Austin Wilson

Snake Season

A snake skin dangles from the branches of a blackgum.
We can rest beneath it, in shade,
escape the present heat.
Somewhere the resurrected snake
suns itself, its new skin glistening like mica.

Above buzzards circle in search patterns,
alert for any sign of death.

The undergrowth is
alive with a snake's curling
to a coil.

The dried gourd of his tail rattles,
gives us time,
before the strike,
to live.

Edward Wilson

Boy

He can hardly walk
but grinning up at us
he's steady on legs
plump as drumsticks.
The first sentence, first
shoelace tied, the first
note he'll learn to whistle
are for the future, over
the horizon. Just now
he's examining the
sidewalk, the beads of
ants like a broken neck-
lace spilling away into
the grass. His mother
has yet to cry for his
first haircut. Just now
those strands lift in the
breeze and the sun
ignites them. Like soft
electricity. Articulate as
spider silk, telling us
what he's thinking, who
he is, when all we have
are words.

Smoke knows

after so long locked
in a stick. It's
just using the fire.
It leaves us
a little whisper. So
we'll remember. So,
when the time comes,
we'll know how.

Ralph Tejeda Wilson

The Little Deaths

Many fingers and many toes, and not at all
that sugared light at the end of a tunnel
certain piggies can't help walking towards.
They also returned. The usual music for alarm,
percolations of soap and coffee, and the toneless charm
of lifting one's chin from bed to board.

As for weather, its black & white: a walk
in the park back into the labyrinth
to discover the grift of one's figment restored
like a credit card others continue to honor.
Is it yours? The future's drift
fingered like a hopeful thread, marks

scored secretly along foretold walls
towards corners where one will turn
& Time hook like a man with horns.
Outside, the clamorous festival
of others released, releasing garlands unto the sea.
Not you, not me.

William Wright

Blonde Mare, Iredell County, NC, 1870–1896

No one thinks of you anymore, your bones now broken
beneath the barn's dark rutted boards, turning
with coal, grass, and stars, those few deathless sovereigns.

Who witnessed you blossoming from the stable's
downslant of light, those mounds of golden hay
and chaff your grainy world until the fields lay open?

They worked you hard, your muscles hauling Scots plow
through furrow, chisel and coulter loosening earth
till dusk. They'd prod you and you'd chuff.

But now they are with you, too, all knitted by death's
twine, your crux not lost but heaved by creek
and meadow, sluiced through the blowing manes of trees.

Caroline Young

Forty

What I first knew of death was the astronaut.

His blue suit, a body blocking my view,
The lecture: the horrible end of the sun.
Red giant, blue dwarf. Which comes first?

It has been too long since you answered me.
Grey hairs pop like weeds in my scalp,
Smoke signals from the chimney.

My mind plants you on the front porch.
I dress you in a bathing suit, dying
For sunlight in February.

What I now know of death is the silence.
The things that never enter.

You were already dying before you became
A poppy tattooed on my spine
For reminder.

People now call me by your name.
It makes them feel close to you
But where does that leave me?

I remember the astronaut's pointer,
The slide show. Images of scorched
And arctic earth. The end of time

I could not comprehend. Your response.

Who can say when the sun dies?
He never addressed the moon.
I still recall the nightmares.

Will the moon rise or walk away?
No more questions.
Is it selfish to want more

Than blown out candles,
The answers you withhold?

It was I who took the pen in hand

To sign your life in the surgeon's charge.
Ten years later, what is left?

Your life becoming mine.

Kevin Young

James Brown at B.B. King's on New Year's Eve

The one thing that can solve most
our problems is dancing. And sweat,
cold or not. And burnt ends
of ribs, or reason, of hair
singed & singing. The hot comb's
caress. Days after
he dies, I see James Brown still
scheduled to play B.B. King's
come New Year's Eve—ringing
it in, us, falling to the floor
like the famous glittering midnight
ball drop, countdown, forehead full
of sweat, *please, please,*
please, please, begging
on his knees. The night
King was killed, shot
by the Memphis moan in a town
where B.B. King sang, Saint
James in Boston tells
the crowd: cool it. A riot
onstage, heartache
rehearsed, practiced, don't dare
be late or miss a note
or you'll find yourself fined
fifty bucks. A fortune. Even
the walls sweat. A God-
father's confirmation suit,
his holler, wide-collared, grits
& greens. Encore. Exhausted
after, collapsed, carried
out, away, off—not on a gurney,
no bedsheet over
his bouffant, conk
shining, but, boots on,
in a cape glittering bright
as midnight, or its train.

Ode to Ol Dirty Bastard

F you. Motor
mouth, clown
of class warfare,

welfare millionaire—
how dare you disappear
when we need your

shimmy shimmy ya
here. Osirus
of this shiznit, your body's

now scattered
on wax. No monument,
no fortune left—

just what you made
& spent, I hope, on skunk
weed & worse. *Good*

morning heartache.
Your carelessness
reminds us how

quick we are
to judge, how
serious things

done become. Dirty
as the south, sweet
as neon cherry pie

filling from a can.
I hear folks still call
your number in Brooklyn

all hours
& ask the sleepy, still
listed Russell Jones

(no relation)
come out & play.
Baby, I got

your money.
Big Baby Jesus, Dirt
McGirt, alias-addict—

of course you can't
be reached—
you're too busy, Rusty,

wigging out, dancing
in a humpsuit & jheri curl
toupee, your tiny,

tacky dreads
hidden, your grill
of gold melted

down to pay off
St. Pete, or Beezlebub,
to buy just one more

dose of freedom.

Relics

from The Ballad of Jim Crow

Hitman Jim figured
he'd retire
& become a lawyer.
He'd barely need

to paint over his old sign
ASSASSIN FOR HIRE.
Above, in white:
James Crow, esquire.

His calling card:
a thousand yard
stare. Judges
didn't scare him

nor could prayer.
On a stack of bibles
he swore.
On his mother's grave

though she breathed
no word of what
she knew he did. He swore
folks to tell the whole—

just as he'd once taken
the Lord's name
in vain. His principle
business: pain.

His clients the weak
& lame, those poor
enough to afford
only to pay him in good

will, or hot food. In gratitude
they named
their children after him,
even a high school—

once the best around,
now turned
into a gym, or jail,
or torn down.

The Poets

HOLLY J. ALDERMAN was born in Bryson City, North Carolina, in 1975. She holds a Bachelor of Arts in Creative Writing from the University of South Florida. She currently resides in Athens, Georgia, where she attends graduate school at the University of Georgia. Alderman is a published song writer.

DIANA ANHALT, author of A *Gathering of Fugitives: Voices of American Political Expatriates in Mexico 1948-1965*, (Archer Books) and a chapbook, *Shiny Objects*, is a former resident of Mexico City, who currently lives in Atlanta, Georgia. Her poetry has appeared in *Nimrod*, *The Comstock Review*, *The Litchfield Review*, *Poetry USA*, *California Quarterly*, *Poem*, and *Atlanta Review*, among others. Future Cycle Press recently released her chapbook, *Second Skin*.

REBECCA BAGGETT has published four poetry collections, the most recent of which are *Thalassa* (Finishing Line Press, 2011) and *God Puts on the Body of a Deer* (Main Street Rag, 2010). Recent work appears in journals including *Atlanta Review*, *Crab Orchard Review*, *Poetry East*, *Southern Poetry Review*, and *The Southern Review*. She lives in Athens, Georgia.

FRED BASSETT is a retired academic who holds a Ph.D. in Biblical Literature from Emory University. His poems have been widely published in journals and anthologies. His latest book of poetry, *The Old Stoic Faces the Mirror*, was published in 2010. His debut novel, *South Wind Rising*, was also published in 2010, and he is currently revising the sequel, *Honey from a Lion*.

KIMBERLY L. BECKER is a member of Wordcraft Circle of Native Writers and Storytellers and author of *Words Facing East* (WordTech Editions, 2011). Recent work appears in *Drunken Boat*, *Future Earth Magazine*, *Sugar Mule*, and *Yellow Medicine Review*.

A poet and Yale-trained Latin American historian, MARJORIE BECKER has published the poetry collections *Piano Glass/Glass Piano* and *Body Bach* and the historical monograph, *Setting the Virgin on Fire*. An Associate Professor of Latin American history and innovative writing at the University of Southern California, her poetry recently has appeared in *Writing on Napkins at the Sunshine Club: An Anthology of Poets Writing in Macon*, *Rethinking History*, *Askew*, *Runes*, and other venues. She once served in the Peace Corps in rural Paraguay.

HANNAH BESSINGER currently writes and lives in Adel, Georgia.

JENN BLAIR's work has appeared in *New South*, *The Tulane Review*, *The James Dickey Review*, *Cold Mountain Review*, and *Copper Nickel*, among others. Her chapbook, *All Things Are Ordered*, is out from Finishing Line Press. She lives in Winterville, Georgia, with her husband and two daughters.

MAGGIE BLAKE, who has lived in six states and two countries, is glad to finally call the South home. She has studied at Stanford, Oxford, and Brown Universities and is now engaged in a five-summer M.F.A. program at Sewanee, the University of the South. Blake is a high school teacher of English in Atlanta.

JULIE E. BLOEMEKE's poems have recently appeared in *A&U: America's AIDS Magazine*, *Qarrtsiluni* and in the collaborative chapbook *Jasper Reads: Download*. Her series of poetry and photography on abandoned spaces was featured in *Deep South Magazine*. Her poetry and non-fiction are forthcoming in a number of anthologies. Her poem, "Pinned," recently received the third place poetry prize in the Artists Embassy International's Dancing Poetry Contest. She is currently working on her second poetry manuscript.

STEPHEN BLUESTONE currently lives and works in New York City. His poems have received numerous awards, among them the *Greensboro Review Poetry Prize* and the *Thomas Merton Prize*. He is the author of *The Laughing Monkeys of Gravity* (1995) and *The Flagrant Dead* (2007), both of which were nominated for the National Book Award.

DAVID BOTTOMS's first book, *Shooting Rats at the Bibb County Dump*, was chosen by Robert Penn Warren as winner of the 1979 Walt Whitman Award of the Academy of American Poets. His poems have appeared widely in magazines such as *The Atlantic Monthly*, *The New Yorker*, *Harper's*, *Poetry*, and *The Paris Review*, as well as in numerous anthologies. He is the author of six other books of poetry, two novels, and a book of essays and interviews. His newest book of poems is *Working the Heavy Bag*.

J.O. BRACHMAN is a graduate student in creative writing at the University of West Georgia and has published in *The Birmingham Poetry Review*. She lives outside of Atlanta.

JESSE BREITE currently lives and teaches high school in Atlanta, Georgia. He was raised in Little Rock, Arkansas, and considers it his home. His work has been published in *Prairie Schooner*, *Prick of the Spindle*, *Slant: A Journal of Poetry*, *Toad*, and *Main Street Rag*. Jesse enjoys spending time with his wife, Emily, and attempts to write a bit each night.

MOLLY BRODAK is the author of *A Little Middle of the Night* (University of Iowa Press, 2010) and the chapbook *The Flood* (Coconut Books, 2012). She lives in Atlanta and edits the journal *Aesthetix*.

JODY BROOKS lives in Atlanta, Georgia. Her short fiction has appeared in *DIAGRAM*, *Knee-Jerk*, *Hobart*, *Monkeybicycle*, and *Hot Metal Bridge*.

BRIAN BROWN is a photographer and documentary historian in Savannah, Georgia. Recent work has appeared in *Chiron Review*, *Keyhole*, *Powhatan Review*, *Town Creek Poetry*, *Homestead Review*, *Flycatcher*, *Roanoke Review*, and *The Civil War in Georgia* (UGA Press), among others. He was 2008 recipient of the Dorothy Sargent Rosenberg Poetry Prize. His website, *Vanishing South Georgia*, focuses on the endangered vernacular architecture and folk culture of his native region; two book projects related to this work will be published in 2013.

STACEY LYNN BROWN was born and raised in Atlanta, Georgia, and received her MFA from The University of Oregon. A poet, playwright, and essayist, her work has appeared in numerous journals and anthologies. She is the author of the book-length poem *Cradle Song* (C&R Press, 2009) and is the co-editor, with Oliver de la Paz, of *A Face to Meet the Faces: An Anthology of Contemporary Persona Poetry*, which was published by The University of Akron Press in 2012.

KATHRYN STRIPLING BYER has published six collections of poetry, five of them in the LSU Press Poetry Series. Her recent volume, *Descent* (LSU, 2012), focuses on her inheritance as a white woman coming of age during the Civil Rights Era. Her poetry, fiction, and essays have appeared in *The Atlantic Monthly*, *Shenandoah*, and *The Georgia Review*, among others, as well as numerous anthologies.

MELISA CAHNMANN-TAYLOR is associate professor in language and literacy education at the University of Georgia. She has published poems and reviews in journals such as *American Poetry Review*, *Quarterly West*, *Puerto del Sol*, *Barrow Street*, *Women's Review of Books*, *Cream City Review*, *The Georgia Review*, and *Literary Mama*. She is the winner of several Dorothy Sargent Rosenberg Prizes and a Leeway Poetry Grant, and has co-authored two books, *Teachers Act Up: Creating Multicultural Learning Communities Through Theatre* (Teachers College Press, 2010) and *Arts-Based Research in Education: Foundations for Practice* (Routledge, 2008).

BRENT CALDERWOOD is Literary Editor of *A&U Magazine* and Associate Editor of *Lambda Literary*. His poems have appeared in *American Poetry Journal*, *Poets & Artists*, *Crab Creek Review*, *The Gay & Lesbian Review Worldwide*, and elsewhere. His poem "The Golden Hour" was selected by Mark Doty as winner of the 2011 Atlanta Queer Literary Festival Broadside Contest. His debut collection, *The God of Longing*, will be published in 2013.

KEVIN CANTWELL's poems have appeared in *Commonweal*, *Poetry*, *The Paris Review*, and *The New Republic*. He won the River City Award in 2001. In 2002, New Issues Press published *Something Black in the Green Part of Your Eye*. *One of Those Russian Novels* was published in 2009, and *Writing on Napkins at the Sunshine Club: An Anthology of Poets Writing in Macon* appeared from Mercer University Press in 2011. He won the James Dickey Award from *Five Points* in 2012.

MICHELLE CASTLEBERRY was born in Texas, grew up in Arkansas on a tomato farm, and moved to Georgia in the mid-nineties. She works as a therapist in Athens, Georgia and lives and writes in nearby Watkinsville. Her work has appeared in journals including *Six Little Things*, *Poemeleon*, *Bellemeade Books*, and *Athens Word of Mouth*.

KATIE CHAPLE is the author of *Pretty Little Rooms* (Press 53, 2011), which won the 2012 Devil's Kitchen Reading Award in Poetry. She is currently the editor of *Terminus Magazine* and teaches poetry and writing at the University of West Georgia. Her work has appeared in such journals as *Antioch Review*, *Birmingham Poetry Review*, *Crab Orchard Review*, *Passages North*, and *Washington Square*.

ELIZABETH J. COLEN was born in the Midwest, has lived in the Northeast and Southeast, and currently makes her home in the Pacific Northwest. She is the author of prose poetry collection *Money for Sunsets* (Steel Toe Books, 2010) and the forthcoming fiction chapbook *Dear Mother Monster, Dear Daughter Mistake* (Rose Metal Press, 2011).

STEPHEN COREY is the author of nine poetry collections, from *The Last Magician* (Water Mark Press, 1981) to his most recent, *There Is No Finished World* (White Pine Press, 2003). He is the editor of *The Georgia Review*, with which he has worked since 1983.

DANIEL CORRIE lives on a farm in Tift County. He has received the Southwest Review's first-place Morton Marr Prize. Other of his poems have appeared in *The American Scholar*, *Hudson Review*, *New Criterion*, *The Southern Review*, and *Virginia Quarterly Review*, among others.

CHAD DAVIDSON is the author of *The Last Predicta* (2008) and *Consolation Miracle* (2003), both from Southern Illinois UP, as well as co-author with Gregory Fraser of *Writing Poetry: Creative and Critical Approaches*, (Palgrave Macmillan, 2009). He is an Associate Professor of Literature and Creative Writing at the University of West Georgia, near Atlanta.

TRAVIS DENTON lives in Atlanta with his daughter Helena Skylark. He is the Associate Director of Poetry @ TECH as well as McEver Chair in Poetry at Georgia Tech. He is also co-founding editor of the literary arts publication, *Terminus Magazine*. His poems have appeared in numerous journals, magazines and anthologies. His collection of poems *The Burden of Speech* was published by C & R press in 2009. His second book, *When Pianos Fall from the Sky* will be published by Marick Press in fall of 2012.

MICHAEL DIEBERT hails from Kingsport, Tennessee, the Model City. He lives in Atlanta, Georgia, where he teaches writing and literature at Georgia Perimeter College and serves as poetry editor for *The Chattahoochee Review*. He is the recipient of a residency from the Writers' Colony at Dairy Hollow in northwest Arkansas. Recent poems have appeared in *RATTLE*, *Southern Poetry Review*, *The Monarch Review*, and *Scythe*.

MAUDELLE DRISKELL, the Executive Director of The Frost Place in Franconia, New Hampshire, holds an M.F.A. in poetry from Warren Wilson College. She is the recipient of the Ruth Lilly Fellowship, awarded by *Poetry* and the Modern Language Association. Her work has appeared in *Poetry*, *Kenyon Review*, *CAIRN*, *New Orleans Review*, *All Shook Up*, *The Made Thing*, *The Cortland Review*, and *Inch*.

BLANCHE FARLEY, of Dublin, Georgia, has published poetry in *Confrontation*, *Southern Poetry Review*, *Tar River Poetry*, and various other journals. Her work is also included in *The Signet Book of American Humor* and *The Bedford Introduction to Literature*. She co-edited a gift anthology, *Like a Summer Peach: Sunbright Poems and Old Southern Recipes* (Papier-Maché Press, 1996). A grouping of her poems, "Grave Numbers," was set to music by composer Clare Shore and was initially performed at Stratford Hall in Washington, D.C.

MALAIKA FAVORITE is a visual artist and writer. Her poetry publication, *Illuminated Manuscript*, was released by New Orleans Poetry Journal Press in 1991. Her poetry, fiction, and articles appear in numerous anthologies and journals, including *Pen International*, *Hurricane Blues*, *Drumvoices Review*, *Uncommon Place*, *Xavier Review*, *The Maple Leaf Rag*, *Visions International*, *Louisiana Literature*, *Louisiana English Journal*, *Big Muddy*, and *Art Papers*.

RUPERT FIKE's collection, *Lotus Buffet*, was published in 2011 by Brick Road Poetry Press. Two of its poems were nominated for a Pushcart Prize, and he was recently named Finalist as Georgia Author of the Year for 2011 in poetry. He has a poem inscribed in a downtown Atlanta plaza, and his non-fiction book, *Voices from The Farm*, accounts of life in a spiritual community in the 1970s, has just been re-issued.

STARKEY FLYTHE, J.R. graduated from the University of the South in Sewanee, Tennessee, served with the army in the Middle East and Africa, and re-founded and served as managing editor of *The Saturday Evening Post* and *Holiday*. His fiction has been anthologized in *The Best American Short Stories*, *New Stories from the South*, and *O. Henry Prize* volumes. He has two books of poetry from Furman University's Ninety-Six Press and one from Snake Nation Press. He won the 2011 *Inkwell* Poetry Prize from Manhattanville College and was co-winner of the *Shenandoah* 60th Anniversary Flannery O'Connor Fiction Prize. The University of Iowa Press published his collection of short fiction in 1990.

ETHAN FOGUS is pursuing a BFA in poetry at Georgia State University. He is currently Associate Editor at *New South: Journal of Art and Literature*. His work has recently appeared in *Curio Poetry* and *Town Creek Poetry*. Ethan lives and works in Atlanta, Georgia.

GREGORY FRASER is the author of three poetry collections: *Strange Pietà* (Texas Tech, 2003), *Answering the Ruins* (Northwestern, 2009), and *Designed for Flight* (Northwestern, 2013). He is also the co-author (with Chad Davidson) of the textbooks *Writing Poetry* (Palgrave Macmillan, 2009) and *Analyze Anything* (Continuum-Bloomsbury, 2012). The recipient of a grant from the National Endowment for the Arts, and the 2010 Georgia Author of the Year in poetry, Fraser teaches Literature and Creative Writing at the University of West Georgia.

KERRI FRENCH's poetry has been featured on SIRIUS Satellite Radio and has appeared or is forthcoming in *Barrow Street*, *The American Poetry Journal*, *Sou'wester*, *The Southeast Review*, *The Pinch*, *Barrelhouse*, *DIAGRAM*, and *Best New Poets 2008*, among others. A North Carolina native, she has lived and worked in Georgia, Massachusetts, and England.

ALICE FRIMAN's newest collection is *Vinculum*, from LSU Press. Friman's work appears in *Best American Poetry 2009*, *The Georgia Review*, *The Gettysburg Review*, *Boulevard*, *New Letters*, and many others. She is a recipient of a 2012 Pushcart Prize and the 2012 Georgia Author of the Year Award for Poetry. Friman lives in Milledgeville, where she is Poet-in-Residence at Georgia College.

ERIN GANAWAY holds a M.F.A. from Hollins University. Her work has appeared or is forthcoming in the *New York Quarterly*, *Third Coast*, *Sea Stories*, and elsewhere. She was a featured poet in *Town Creek Poetry*, and her poem was selected for inclusion in *Best New Poets*. She divides her time between Atlanta and Cape Cod.

MAC GAY was born in Atlanta, Georgia, in 1948. He received both his B.S. and M.S. in biology from the University of Georgia. He is the author of two chapbooks, *Dearests*, and *Physical Science*, which won the Tennessee Chapbook Prize in 2003. A full length collection, *Anecdotal Evidence*, is currently seeking a home. He has worked as a carpenter and teacher and is currently an Adjunct Professor in Ccience at Georgia Perimeter College.

ROBERTA GEORGE founded Snake Nation Press in 1989 and later served at the Lowndes/Valdosta Arts Commission as Executive Director for ten years, doing everything from painting walls to writing grants. This past year George has won prizes for stories from her collection *Below the Gnat Line*. She recently had two poems accepted by the *Southern Poetry Review* and by *The New Guard* and won a first prize from the Porter Fleming Foundation for her short story, *Petty Crimes*.

SARAH GORDON of Athens, Georgia, is the author of *Distances* (Brito & Lair, 1999) and has published poetry in *The Georgia Review, Shenandoah, Southern Poetry Review, Apalachee Quarterly, Confrontation, Calyx*, and elsewhere. She is the author of *Flannery O'Connor: The Obedient Imagination* (Georgia, 2003) and *A Reader's Guide to Flannery O'Connor's Georgia* (Georgia, 2008).

G.R. GREENBAUM is a member of The Poetry Group and The Authors Club in Augusta, Georgia, both comprised of published writers. A retired educator, most recently from Augusta State University, Greenbaum taught in the humanities. Presently, she is a docent at The Morris Museum of Art. She is married to Dr. Lowell Greenbaum, a mother of three children, and grandmother of nine.

SIÂN GRIFFITHS's work is published in *Quarterly West, Ninth Letter, Cave Wall, Permafrost, Versal, Court Green*, and *The Georgia Review*, among other publications. Her story "What Is Solid" was nominated for a Pushcart Prize, and Janet Burroway included her poem, "Fistful," in the third edition of *Imaginative Writing*. Her first novel, *Borrowed Horses*, is forthcoming from New Rivers Press.

ANTHONY GROOMS was educated at the College of William and Mary and George Mason University. He is the author of *Ice Poems*, a chapbook, *Trouble No More: Stories*, and *Bombingham*, a novel. His work appears in *Callaloo, African American Review, Crab Orchard Review, George Washington Review*, and others. He is a Fulbright Fellow, a Finalist for the Legacy Award from Hurston-Wright Foundation, an Arts Administration Fellow from the National Endowment for the Arts, and the recipient of two Lillian Smith Prizes from the Southern Regional Council.

LINDA LEE HARPER's most recent full-length collection, *Kiss Kiss*, won the Open Competition of Cleveland State University Poetry Center. With four Pushcart nominations, one previous collection *Toward Desire*, seven chapbooks, including *Blue Flute* from Adastra Press, and three Yaddo fellowships, Harper has published in over ninety literary journals, including *The Georgia Review, Nimrod*, and *Rattle*. She lives in Augusta, Georgia.

KAREN HEAD is the author of *Sassing* (WordTech Press, 2009), *My Paris Year* (All Nations Press, 2009) and *Shadow Boxes* (All Nations Press, 2003). Her digital project *Poetic Rub* was featured at E-Poetry-2007 in Paris. Another digital project involved a collaborative exquisite corpse created via Twitter with twelve other poets while she stood atop the Fourth Plinth in Trafalgar Square as part of Antony Gormley's *One and Other Project*; "Monumental" was detailed in a *TIME* online mini-documentary. She's an Atlanta native.

M. AYODELE HEATH is author of *Otherness* (Brick Road Poetry Press). His awards include an Atlanta Bureau for Cultural Affairs Emerging Artist Grant. He is a Pushcart Prize nominee and the McEver Visiting Chair in Writing at Georgia Tech. He earned a fellowship to the Caversham Centre for Artists (South Africa), and was top-10 finalist at the National Poetry Slam. His poetry has appeared in *Crab Orchard Review, Mississippi Review, Badilisha Poetry, India's International Gallerie*, and the anthology *Poetry Slam: the Competitive Art of Performance Poetry*.

SARA HENNING's poetry, fiction, interviews and book reviews have appeared in such journals as *Verse, So To Speak, Weave*, and *The Sow's Ear Poetry Review*. Her chapbook, *To Speak of Dahlias*, is forthcoming from Finishing Line Press. Currently a doctoral student in English and Creative Writing at the University of South Dakota, she serves as Associate Poetry Editor of *The South Dakota Review*.

LISA HODGENS lives in the foothills of the Blue Ridge Mountains near the Soque River. She is Professor of English at Piedmont College of Demorest, Georgia. In addition to teaching, she is working on the next poems in the *Riverstone* series and an essay on Lillian Smith and Screamer Mountain.

KAREN PAUL HOLMES divides her time between Atlanta and the North Georgia mountains. Publishing credits include *Poetry East, Atlanta Review, Caesura, Avocet, Your Daily Poem, The Sow's Ear Poetry Review* and the upcoming anthology, *American Society: What Poets See* by FutureCycle Press. A former VP-Communications at ING, Karen now leads a kinder, gentler life as a freelance writer and poet. She founded/hosts a poetry critique group in Atlanta and Writers' Night Out in Hiawassee.

RANDALL HORTON is the author of *The Definition of Place* and the *Lingua Franca of Ninth Street*, both from Main Street Rag. Randall's awards include a National Endowment of the Arts Fellowship in Literature. Triquarterly/ Northwestern University Press will publish his latest poetry collection *Pitch Dark Anarchy* in Spring 2013.

JAMES HUDSON is an Emeritus Professor of Medicine at the Medical College of Georgia. which he joined in 1961. He was born in New York, went to New York City public schools, Dartmouth College (A.B.) and Boston University (M.D.). His poetry has appeared in magazines, and in periodicals of The Georgia Poetry Society and The Poetry Society of South Carolina.

T.R. HUMMER's twelfth book, *Ephemeron* (poems), was published by LSU Press's Southern Messenger Series in Fall 2011; Hummer teaches in the Creative Writing Program at Arizona State University. Hummer was the Editor-in-Chief of *The Georgia Review* from 2001-2006, during which time he lived in Athens, GA. Hummer is also a musician; a new CD, *AmeriCamera part I: High Minded* was just issued in a pre-release limited edition, with songs he co-wrote with his collaborator, Billy Cioffi.

MIKE JAMES's work has been widely published in magazines throughout the country. His seventh and most recent poetry collection is *Past Due Notices: Poems 1991-2011* (Main Street Rag, 2012) After years spent in Kansas City, Missouri, and Pittsburgh, Pennsylvania, he now lives in Douglasville, Georgia with his wife and five children.

CHRISTOPHER JELLEY was born in Welwyn Garden City, England. Emigrating to Atlanta in 1968, he studied journalism at Georgia State University. Jelley has written scripts for travel and instructional videos and commercials. He lived for several years in the mountains of Tennessee and currently resides in Monroe, Georgia.

A Georgia native and the former director of the Georgia Poetry Circuit, GORDON JOHNSTON's chapbook *Gravity's Light Grip* (Perkolator Press, 2008) was illustrated by Amy Pirkle. Gordon fires his poems onto clay tiles and bottles in the anagama kiln of Roger Jamison in Juliette, Georgia. Gordon has had poems, stories, interviews and essays in *The Georgia Review, Arts & Letters, Many Mountains Moving, Third Genre, Atlanta Review, Denver Quarterly*, and other publications. He teaches Creative Writing and Contemporary Letters at Mercer University in Macon, Georgia.

SEABORN JONES has published two full-length books, *Drowning from the Inside Out* and *Lost Keys*, and three chapbooks, *X-Ray Movies, Black Champagne*, and *Getaway Car in Reverse*. His most recent volume, *Going Farther into the Woods than the Woods Go*, won Mercer University's Adrienne Bond Award. He has published in numerous journals, such as *The New York Quarterly, River Styx*, and *Southern Poetry Review*. His honors include two Individual Artist Awards from the Georgia Arts Council, the Georgia Author of the Year Award in poetry, the Violet Reed Haas Poetry award, and selection as a Bread Loaf scholar. A former Marine, he has worked as a lighting director for *Mr. Rogers' Neighborhood of Make-believe*, is a certified zoo curator, and occasionally teaches poetry through the Bibb County Arts Institute, Macon, Georgia.

MELANIE JORDAN's chapbook, *Ghost Season*, is available from Ropewalk Press. Her poems have appeared or are forthcoming in *Iowa Review, Hayden's Ferry Review, Black Warrior Review, Diagram, Crab Orchard Review, Third Coast, Southeast Review, Poetry Southeast, Sou'wester*, and others. She teaches Creative Writing, Literature, and Composition at the University of West Georgia.

PAT LANDRETH KELLER has published in a number of literary journals and has received an Individual Writer's Award from the Georgia Council for the Arts. Toadlily Press published her chapbook, *Draglines*, and her work is included in *The Best of Toadlily Press*.

COLLIN KELLEY is the author of the novels *Conquering Venus* and *Remain In Light*, which was a 2012 finalist for the Townsend Prize for Fiction. His poetry collections include *Better To Travel, Slow To Burn, After the Poison* and *Render*. His poetry, interviews and essays have appeared in magazines around the world.

ANTHONY KELLMAN is Professor of Creative Writing at Augusta State University, Georgia. He's the author of five books of poetry, including *Limestone*, an epic poem (2008). A new collection, *South Eastern Stages*, is forthcoming in 2012. His novels are *The Coral Rooms* and *The Houses of Alphonso*. Born in Barbados, he is a recipient of a USA National Endowment for the Arts fellowship. His work regularly appears in international magazines and anthologies.

BILL KING lived in Athens, Georgia, from 1983-1996. He now teaches at Davis & Elkins College in Elkins, West Virginia, where he directs the D&E Writers' Series. His work has appeared in such journals as *Mississippi Quarterly, XCP: Cross-Cultural Poetics, Still: The Journal, Nantahala: A Review of Writing and Photography in Appalachia*, and others.

DAVID KING is Associate Professor of English and Film Studies at Kennesaw State University, where he has taught for twenty years. His poetry has appeared in several magazines, and he has won first prize awards from both The Academy of American Poets and The Poetry Society of America. He is also an award-winning contributing literature and film columnist for *The Georgia Bulletin*, the newspaper of the Roman Catholic Archdiocese of Atlanta.

HILARY KING lives in Atlanta, Georgia. Her poems have appeared in *The Cortland Review, Blue Fifth Review, PANK, Gertrude, Vinyl Poetry, Bumble Jacket Miscellany* and other publications.

ALYSE KNORR's first book, *Annotated Glass*, is forthcoming from Furniture Press Books in 2014. Knorr's work has appeared or is forthcoming in *Gargoyle, Sentence, Puerto Del Sol*, and *RHINO*. She is co-founding editor of Gazing Grain Press and serves as production director of the Fall for the Book Literary Festival.

ROBERT KRUT is the author of *The Spider Sermons* (BlazeVox, 2009). His poems have appeared in *The Cimarron Review, Blackbird, Smartish Pace, The Mid-American Review*, and more. He teaches at the University of California, Santa Barbara; previously, he lived in Atlanta and taught at Georgia State University.

JOSHUA LAVENDER grew up traipsing across the fields and backroads of southern Georgia. He earned a B.A. in English Literature at Georgia College & State University in Milledgeville, then picked guitar for a while in east Tennessee. Presently, he is attending the M.F.A. Poetry program at the University of Maryland, College Park.

KATHLEEN BREWIN LEWIS's prose, poetry, and prose poetry has appeared in *Weave, Boston Literary Magazine, The Prose-Poem Project, Deep South Magazine, Constellations, Loose Change, Slice of Life*, and *a handful of stones*. She has an M.A. in Professional Writing from Kennesaw State University and is the Senior Editor of an online literary journal, *Flycatcher: A Journal of Native Imagination*. Born and raised in Savannah, Kathleen now lives in Atlanta with her family.

CODY LUMPKIN was born in north Georgia around hog-killing time. He earned his Ph.D. in English from the University of Nebraska-Lincoln and currently serves as a Visiting Assistant Professor in English at Marshall University in West Virginia.

THOMAS LUX, author of many books of poems, is the Bourne Chair in Poetry and the director of the McEver Visiting Writers Program at the Georgia Institute of Technology. He has been awarded several NEA grants, the Kingsley Tufts Award, and is a former Guggenheim Fellow. He lives in Atlanta.

DAN MARSHALL is a lecturer at Georgia State University in Atlanta. His fiction has appeared in *Hot Metal Bridge* and *Terminus*. "Koan" is part of a larger project of linked prose poems called *Firelands*.

CHRISTOPHER MARTIN is author of the poetry chapbook *A Conference of Birds* (New Native Press, 2012). His work has appeared or is forthcoming in *Shambhala Sun, Ruminate, Drafthorse, Still: The Journal, Poecology, Buddhist Poetry Review, Thrush, Town Creek Poetry, Loose Change*, and elsewhere. The founding editor of *Flycatcher* and a contributing editor for *New Southerner*, Martin lives with his wife and their two children in the northwest Georgia piedmont, between the Allatoona Range and Kennesaw Mountain.

JAMES MAY served as the editor-in-chief of *New South* from 2008 until 2011. Currently the writer-in-residence at Agnes Scott College, he lives in Decatur, Georgia, with his wife, the poet Chelsea Rathburn.

MARIANA MCDONALD is a bicultural poet whose poetry has appeared in numerous publications, including *Sugar Mule, From a Bend in the River: 100 New Orleans Poets, Jambalaya, The Guardian*, and *El Boletín Nacional*. She lives in Atlanta, where she is active in the poetry community. She works as a Public Health Scientist addressing health disparities.

SANDRA MEEK is the author of four books of poems, *Road Scatter* (Persea Books, 2012), the Dorset Prize-winning *Biogeography* (Tupelo, 2008), *Burn* (2005), and *Nomadic Foundations* (2002), and editor of *Deep Travel: Contemporary American Poets Abroad* (Ninebark, 2007). A 2011 NEA awardee and twice-named Georgia Author of the Year for poetry, Meek is director of the Georgia Poetry Circuit, poetry editor for *Phi Kappa Phi Forum*, co-founding editor of Ninebark Press, and Dana Professor of English at Berry College.

JUDSON MITCHAM's work has appeared in many literary journals, including *The Georgia Review, Poetry, Hudson Review*, and *Harper's*. He has published three collections of poems: *Somewhere in Ecclesiastes*, which won the Devins Award; *This April Day*; and *A Little Salvation: Poems Old and New*. His novels, *The Sweet Everlasting* and *Sabbath Creek*, were both awarded the Townsend Prize for Fiction. Mitcham taught psychology at Fort Valley State University for many years, and he currently teaches writing at Mercer University and in the M.F.A. program at Georgia College. He is the current Poet Laureate of Georgia.

MAREN O. MITCHELL's poems have appeared in *Southern Humanities Review, The Journal of Kentucky Studies, Wild Goose Poetry Review, The Classical Outlook, Appalachian Journal, The Arts Journal, Echoes Across the Blue Ridge, Nurturing Paws*, and elsewhere. Poems are forthcoming in *Pirene's Fountain, Wild Goose Poetry Review, The Journal of Kentucky Studies*, and *Japan Anthology*. She lives in the mountains of north Georgia with her husband and two cats.

JANICE TOWNLEY MOORE, a native of Atlanta, is Associate Professor of English at Young Harris College. Her chapbook, *Teaching the Robins*, was published by Finishing Line Press, and in 2009 she won first place in poetry in Press 53 Open Awards. Her poems have appeared in *The Georgia Review, Prairie Schooner, Southern Poetry Review, Connecticut Review*, among others. Recently she published an article in *The Flannery O'Connor Review*.

TONY MORRIS has published three collections of poems: *Fugue's End* (Birch Brook Press, 2004), *Back to Cain* (The Olive Press, 2006), and *Greatest Hits* (Puddinghouse Press, 2012). His work has appeared in various journals, including: *Spoon River Poetry Review, Hawai'i Review, Southern Poetry Review, River Styx, South Dakota Review, Connecticut Review, Green Mountains Review*, and many others. He is also the managing editor of *Southern Poetry Review*, and the director of the Ossabaw Island Writers' Retreat.

GINGER MURCHISON, together with Thomas Lux, founded Georgia Tech's POETRY @ TECH, where she served as associate director five years and has been one of its McEver Visiting Chairs in Poetry since 2009. A three-time Pushcart nominee, she is a graduate of Warren Wilson's M.F.A. Program for Writers and editor of the acclaimed *Cortland Review*. Her first chapbook of poems, *Out Here*, was published by Jeanne Duval Editions in 2008.

ALICIA REBECCA MYERS received her M.F.A. in poetry from New York University, where she was a Goldwater Writing Fellow. Her chapbook of poems, *Greener*, was released from Finishing Line Press in 2009. She has work forthcoming in *Creative Non-Fiction* and *Cream City Review*, and mostly recently taught at the Iowa Young Writers' Studio and the Iowa Summer Writing Festival. She lives in Athens, Georgia, with poet Dan Rosenberg and works as a travel consultant specializing in Disney vacations.

ERIC NELSON's five poetry collections include *The Twins* (2009), winner of the Split Oak Press Chapbook Award; *Terrestrials* (2004), winner of the X.J. Kennedy Poetry Award; and *The Interpretation of Waking Life* (1991), winner of the Arkansas Poetry Award. His poems have appeared in *Poetry, The Cincinnati Review, The Southern Review, The Oxford American, The Sun*, and many other venues. He teaches at Georgia Southern University.

ROBERT PARHAM is co-editor of the *Southern Poetry Review*. He has published poetry in *The Georgia Review*, *The Southern Review*, *Shenandoah*, and numerous other journals. He has also published several chapbooks. He recently retired as Dean of Arts and Sciences at Augusta State University.

AMY PENCE is the author of the poetry collections *Armor, Amour* (Ninebark Press, 2012), *The Decadent Lovely* (Main Street Rag, 2010) and the chapbook *Skin's Dark Night* (2River Press, 2003). Her poems have appeared in a wide variety of publications, including *New American Writing*, *The Oxford American*, *The Antioch Review*, and *Quarterly West*. Her fiction and nonfiction have been published in *Silk Road*, *Poets & Writers*, and *The Writer's Chronicle*, among others.

PATRICIA PERCIVAL is a graduate of Duke University and Emory University School of Law. Her work has been published in *phati'tude Literary Magazine*, *Stonepile Writer's Anthology: Volume II*, the anthology *Sunrise from Blue Thunder*, published by Pirene's Fountain, and in *Town Creek Poetry*.

PATRICK PHILLIPS is currently a fellow of the John Simon Guggenheim Memorial Foundation. His first book, *Chattahoochee*, received the 2005 Kate Tufts Discovery Award, and his second, *Boy*, was published by the University of Georgia Press in 2008. His poems have appeared in many magazines, including *Poetry*, *Ploughshares*, and *The Nation*, and he has received support from the National Endowment for the Arts, the U.S. Fulbright Commission, and the Bread Loaf Writers' Conference. He lives in Brooklyn and teaches at Drew University.

DAVID SCOTT POINTER was nominated for three Pushcart Prizes in 2010. Previously, he resided in Albany, Georgia, while serving in the United States Marine Corps in the military police. Recent anthology acceptances include a parenthood anthology at Aortic Books. In 2009, David was declared a winning writer in *Empty Shoes: Poems on Hunger and Homelessness*. *Empty Shoes* is available at Amazon.com and www.popcornpress.com.

STEPHEN ROGER POWERS is the author of *The Follower's Tale*, a collection of poems inspired by Dolly Parton and published by Salmon Poetry in 2009. His second collection, *Hello, Stephen*, is forthcoming from Salmon in 2014. Other work has appeared in *Shenandoah*, *Margie*, and *32 Poems*. He is Associate Professor of English at Gordon College in Georgia.

WYATT PRUNTY, author of many books of poetry, all published by Johns Hopkins University Press, has received Guggenheim, Rockefeller, Johns Hopkins, and Brown Foundation fellowships, and is a member of the Fellowship of Southern Writers. He founded and directs the Sewanee Writers' Conference.

CHELSEA RATHBURN is the author of two poetry collections, *A Raft of Grief* and *The Shifting Line*. Her poems have appeared in *Poetry*, *The Atlantic Monthly*, *Ploughshares* and *The New England Review*, among many other journals. The recipient of a 2009 poetry fellowship from the National Endowment for the Arts, she lives in Decatur, Georgia, with her husband, the poet James May, and their daughter.

Writer, naturalist, and activist JANISSE RAY is author of five books of literary nonfiction, including the latest, *The Seed Underground: A Growing Revolution to Save Food*, as well as a collection of nature poetry, *A House of Branches*. She lives on an organic farm in southern Georgia.

BILLY REYNOLDS was born and raised in Huntsville, Alabama. His awards include the Tennessee Williams scholarship in poetry from the Sewanee Writers' Conference and the John Ciardi scholar in poetry from Bread Loaf Writers' Conference. His poems have been published in *Iron Horse Literary Review*, *Hunger Mountain*, *Sewanee Theological Review*, and *Third Coast*, among others. Currently, he lives in Tifton, Georgia, where he serves as the head of the Department of Literature and Language at Abraham Baldwin Agricultural College.

JONATHAN RICE's poems have been published in *AGNI Online*, *American Literary Review*, *Colorado Review*, *Sycamore Review*, and *Witness*, among others, and included in *A Face to Meet the Faces: An Anthology of Contemporary Persona Poetry*, *Dzanc Books Best of the Web 2009*, and *Best New Poets 2008*. His poetry was also selected for the 2010 *Indiana Review* Poetry Prize, the 2010 Richard Peterson Poetry Prize from *Crab Orchard Review*, the 2008 *Gulf Coast* Poetry Prize, the 2008 Milton-Kessler Memorial Prize from *Harpur Palate*, the 2008 Yellowwood Poetry Prize from *Yalobusha Review*, and the 2006 AWP Intro to Journals Awards.

In addition to having journalism credits, ANN RITTER received an artist-initiated grant in writing from the Georgia Council for the Arts. She has published fiction, essays, and poetry in *Charleston*, *Confrontation*, *GSU Review* (recently renamed *New South*), *Earth's Daughters-flesh and spirit*, *THEMA: Your Reality or Mine*, and *Georgia Journal*. One of her poems was anthologized in *Like a Summer Peach: Sunbright Poems and Old Southern Recipes*.

LIZ ROBBINS's second full collection, *Play Button*, won the 2010 Cider Press Review Book Award, judged by Patricia Smith. Her chapbook, *Girls Turned Like Dials*, won the 2012 YellowJacket Press Prize. Her poems are in recent or forthcoming issues of *Cimarron Review*, *Hayden's Ferry Review*, *The Journal*, *New York Quarterly*, and *Notre Dame Review*. She's an Associate Professor of Creative Writing at Flagler College in St. Augustine, Florida.

DAN ROSENBERG's first book, *The Crushing Organ*, won the 2011 *American Poetry Journal* Book Prize and was published by Dream Horse Press in 2012. His poetry, reviews, and translations have appeared in such magazines as *The Iowa Review*, *jubilat*, *Kenyon Review Online*, and *American Letters & Commentary*. A Ph.D. student at the University of Georgia, he is a co-editor of *Transom*.

ROSEMARY RHODES ROYSTON's chapbook *Splitting the Soil* is forthcoming in 2012 by Redneck Press. She holds an M.F.A. in Writing from Spalding University and is a lecturer at Young Harris College. Royston's poetry has been published in journals such as *The Comstock Review*, *Main Street Rag*, *Coal Hill Review*, *FutureCycle*, and *Alehouse*. Her essays on writing poetry are included in *Women and Poetry: Tips on Writing, Teaching and Publishing by Successful Women Poets*, published McFarland.

JENNY SADRE-ORAFAI is the author of the chapbooks *Weed Over Flower*, *What Her Hair Says About Her*, *Dressing the Throat Plate*, and *Avoid Disaster*. Recent poetry and prose has appeared in *RHINO*, *The Rumpus*, *The Los Angeles Review*, and *South Loop Review*. She is Atlanta Regional Editor for *Coldfront Magazine* and is co-founding editor of *The Night Outside* and *Josephine Quarterly*. Sadre-Orafai is an Assistant Professor of English at Kennesaw State University.

ANGELLE SCOTT is currently a Writing Center Instructional Assistant and an Instructor of English at Dillard University in New Orleans, Louisiana. She has a M.A. and a B.A. in English from the University of New Orleans. Her areas of interest include Creative Writing, American Literature, and Rhetoric and Composition. Her work has been published in *Callaloo*, *Fourteen Hills*, *Black Magnolias Literary Journal*, *Journal of College Writing*, *Flywheel Magazine*, *furiction:review*, and *Pure Slush*, among others.

M.E. SILVERMAN, editor of *Blue Lyra Review*, has appeared in over fifty publications including: *Crab Orchard Review*, *32 Poems*, *Chicago Quarterly Review*, *BatterSea Review*, *The Southern Poetry Anthology*, *The Los Angeles Review*, *Pacific Review*, *Sugar House Review*, and other magazines. M. E. Silverman was a finalist for the 2008 *New Letters* Poetry Award, the 2008 DeNovo Contest and the 2009 *Naugatuck River Review* Contest. He is working on editing a contemporary Jewish anthology with Deborah Ager (Continuum, 2013) and a member of the board of *32 Poems*.

JAMES MALONE SMITH is co-editor of *Southern Poetry Review* and editor of the anthology *Don't Leave Hungry: Fifty Years of Southern Poetry Review* (University of Arkansas Press, 2009). Poems in *AGNI Online*, *Atlanta Review*, *Connecticut Review*, *Nebraska Review*, *Poet Lore*, *Prairie Schooner*, *Quarterly West*, *Shenandoah*, *Tar River Poetry*, and others. Professor of English at Armstrong Atlantic State University in Savannah, he teaches Creative Writing and American Literature. He grew up in the mountains of north Georgia.

LEON STOKESBURY teaches in the Graduate Writing Program at Georgia State University in Atlanta. His first book, *Often in Different Landscapes*, was a co-winner of the first AWP Poetry Competition in 1975. His *Autumn Rhythm: New & Selected Poems* was awarded The Poets' Prize in 1996. He also edited *The Made Thing: An Anthology of Contemporary Southern Poetry*. His poem, "Watching My Mother Take Her Last Breath," was awarded a Pushcart Prize in 2011.

ALICE TEETER studied writing at Eckerd College with Peter Meinke. Her chapbook, entitled *20 CLASS A*, was published in 1975 by Morningstar Media (editors Dorothy Allison, Flo Hollis, Morgan Gwenwald), Tallahassee, FL. Teeter's collection of poems, entitled *String Theory*, won the Georgia Poetry Society's 2008 Charles B. Dickson Chapbook Contest, judged by Lewis Turco. Her book *When It Happens To You. . .* was published in 2009 by Star Cloud Press.

KATHLEEN THOMPSON is a cross-genre writer who has two poetry chapbooks and one full-length poetry book published. She holds an M.F.A. in Writing from Spalding University. She attended a CNF workshop in Paris with Spalding in July 2012. As a speaker ("Road Scholar") with Alabama Humanities Foundation, she offers both a poetry workshop and a fiction lecture.

NATASHA TRETHEWEY, appointed United States Poet Laureate in 2012, received the Pulitzer Prize for Poetry for *Native Guard*, published by Houghton Mifflin in 2007. She holds the Phillis Wheatley Distinguished Chair in Poetry at Emory University and is the Louis D. Rubin Writer-in-Residence for 2012 at Hollins University.

RACHEL TROUSDALE received her Ph.D. from Yale and is now Associate Professor of English at Agnes Scott College in Decatur, Georgia. Her poems have appeared in *Literary Imagination*, *Atlanta Review*, *RHINO*, *Natural Bridge*, *The New Promised Land*, and *Light*, among other places. Her critical book *Nabokov, Rushdie, and the Transnational Imagination* was published by Palgrave Macmillan in 2010.

MEMYE CURTIS TUCKER's collection, *The Watchers* (Ohio U. Press 1998, Hollis Summers Poetry Prize), was named in 2010 one of "The 25 Books All Georgians Should Read" by the Georgia Center for the Book. Poems have also appeared in three prizewinning chapbooks; *Colorado Review*, *The Georgia Review*, *Poetry Daily*, *Shenandoah*, *The Southern Review*, and others; as art song; and abroad in translation. A native Georgian and recipient of the Georgia Writers Association's Lifetime Achievement Award, she teaches poetry writing and is a Senior Editor of *Atlanta Review*.

MIMI VAQUER's poetry and short fiction has appeared or will soon appear in such journals as *Cream City Review*, *Hayden's Ferry Review*, *Gargoyle Magazine*, and *PANK* among others. Her poetry chapbook, *Scratching Bones*, is available through Pudding House Press. She also teaches 10th grade English and serves on the board of the Poetry Society of Georgia. She lives with her husband and two cats in downtown Savannah, Georgia.

KEVIN VAUGHN is a doctoral student in English Literature and Creative Writing at the University of Georgia. He holds an M.F.A. in Poetry from Columbia University and is a fellow of the Cave Canem Foundation. His work has appeared in *Mississippi Review* and *Mythium Literary Journal* among others and has appeared or is upcoming in the anthologies: *The Chemistry of Color* and *Bloodlines: Poems about Murder*. Vaughn is a former Fulbright Research Fellow to Jagiellonian University in Poland.

DAN VEACH, founder and editor of *Atlanta Review*, is the author of *Elephant Water: Poems & ink paintings* (Finishing Line Press, 2012). Winner of the Willis Barnstone Prize, he is co-editor and translator of *Flowers of Flame* (Michigan State University Press, 2008), the first anthology of Iraqi war poetry and winner of an Independent Publisher Book Award.

WILLIAM WALSH has published *Speak So I Shall Know Thee: Interviews with Southern Writers*, *The Ordinary Life of a Sculptor*, *The Conscience of My Other Being*, *Under the Rock Umbrella: Contemporary American Poets from 1951-1977*, and *David Bottoms: Critical Essays and Interviews*. His work has appeared in the *AWP Chronicle*, *Five Points*, *Flannery O'Connor Review*, *James Dickey Review*, *The Kenyon Review*, *Michigan Quarterly Review*, *North American Review*, *Poets & Writers*, *Rattle*, *Shenandoah*, and *Valparaiso Review*.

BETSY WEIR lives and writes in McDuffie County, Georgia near the city of Thomson with her husband, David. She has published poetry in *Atlanta Review*, *Kennesaw Caring Journal*, *Inkling*, *Sand Hills Literary Magazine*, and others. Weir has won awards from The Porter Fleming Writing Competition in both poetry and creative non-fiction, as well as from *Atlanta Review* and *Kennesaw Caring Review*. She is a member of the Augusta Wednesday Poetry Group and Authors Club of Augusta.

KELLY WHIDDON's first poetry collection, *The House Began to Pitch*, from Mercer University Press, recently received the Adrienne Bond Award. Whiddon received her Ph.D. in English/Creative Writing from the Florida State University in 2002 and has published poetry in *Crab Orchard Review*, *Poetry International*, *Southern Poetry Review*, and *Slipstream*, among others. She is currently the President of the Board of Directors for the Georgia Writers' Association and was a Founding Member of the Executive Board for the Crossroads Writers Conference.

AUSTIN WILSON was born and raised in Waycross, Georgia. After teaching at Georgia and what was then called Memphis State, he attended the University of South Carolina (Ph.D., 1974), where James Dickey directed his dissertation, His work has appeared in *Poem*, *Southern Humanities Review*, *Wind*, *Descant*, *Mississippi Review*, *New Orleans Review*, among others. In 2009 he retired after a thirty-three year career at Millsaps College in Jackson, Mississippi, and recently received a fellowship in poetry from the Mississippi Arts Commission.

EDWARD WILSON has degrees from Eckerd College and University of Florida. He has taught at several colleges and universities and, in between, was a financial consultant and worked for the Federal Reserve Bank of Atlanta. He has served on panels for state and local arts councils, and as a visiting artist. He is a recipient of an NEA Fellowship. His work has appeared in *Poetry*, *American Poetry Review*, and the *Southern Poetry Review*, among others. He lives in Augusta, Georgia.

RALPH TEJEDA WILSON teaches at Kennesaw State University and is a member of the graduate faculty of the Master of Arts in Professional Writing program. He was awarded the Georgia Author of the Year Award for Poetry 2002 for his first book, *A Black Bridge* (University of Nevada Press). He has published work in *The New England Review*, *The Georgia Review*, *Prairie Schooner*, *North American Review*, and others.

WILLIAM WRIGHT has published six collections of poems, including the recent *Night Field Anecdote* (Louisiana Literature Press, 2011) and *Bledsoe* (Texas Review Press, 2011). His work has appeared in such journals as *Shenandoah*, *AGNI*, *Connecticut Review*, *New Orleans Review*, *Beloit Poetry Journal*, *The Antioch Review*, *Indiana Review*, *North American Review*, and others. Founder of *Town Creek Poetry* and editor-in-chief of Batture Willow Press, Wright is series editor of *The Southern Poetry Anthology*. Wright recently won the Porter Fleming Prize in Poetry.

CAROLINE YOUNG is a poet and Ph.D. candidate at the University of Georgia. Her work has appeared in *The Carolina Quarterly*, *Southern Women's Review*, *Marco Polo Arts Mag*, and *Real Poetik*. Her first manuscript, *catastrophiliac*, is actively seeking its home.

KEVIN YOUNG is the author of seven books of poetry, including *Ardency: A Chronicle of the Amistad Rebels*, winner of the American Book Award, and *Jelly Roll: A Blues*, which was a finalist for the National Book Award and the Los Angeles Times Book Prize and won the Paterson Poetry Prize. He is the editor of eight other collections, most recently *Collected Poems of Lucille Clifton 1965-2010* (edited with Michael S. Glaser). *The Grey Album: On the Blackness of Blackness*, won the Graywolf Press Nonfiction Prize and appeared in March 2012. His family hails from Louisiana, where they have lived for two hundred years; all told, he has lived in Georgia longer than he's lived anywhere else. He is a curator and Atticus Haygood Professor at Emory University.

Acknowledgements

Space limitations preclude a full acknowledgments addendum, but the editors wish to thank the myriad journals in which many of the poems of this anthology first appeared. Texas Review Press has been granted permission to print all poems included herein; all rights revert to respective authors. A special thanks to Michelle Nichols Wright, who helped proofread this anthology.